Humor
Theory
Formula of Laughter

IGOR KRICHTAFOVITCH

Outskirts Press, Inc.
Denver, Colorado

Humor Theory
Formula of Laughter

Outskirts Press
http://www.outskirtspress.com

ISBN 10: 1-59800-222-8
ISBN 13: 978-1-59800-222-5

Outskirts Press and the "OP" logo are trademarks belonging to
Outskirts Press, Inc.

Printed in the United States of America

Humor Theory

*The desire to write about funny is evidence
that the sense of humor is lost to us for good.*

Bernard Shaw

Table of Contents

IGOR KRICHTAFOVITCH

HUMOR
THEORY

ILLUSTRATED BY YURI IVANOV

2005

Authorized translation by **Anna Tonkonogui**

Foreword

If one dares to proclaim in earnest that laughter is as necessary to human survival as the instinct of self-preservation or sex, he risks becoming an object of public ridicule.

Jokes, anecdotes, farces, and caricatures are treated as things of a secondary importance in our society; as things not particularly significant to our daily lives or to the path of the development of history. But if the nonbiased reader takes this issue under critical observation, he will undoubtedly see the errors in this curbed position.

How long can someone survive without food or drink? Intervals between the intake of sustenance usually last several hours, but can be stretched to tens of days without particular harm to one's health. A person can go without drinking for a considerable while. People can abstain from sex for some time, sometimes for hours. There are people, including those of inordinate talent and genius, who have never had sexual relations.

But can we find people who have never laughed? Doubtless, even if such people could be found, their numbers would be much smaller than those of virgins.

How frequently do we laugh? Once in a month? Once per week?

Humans come across something funny or make something

humorous up themselves daily, several times a day, frequently tens of times per day. We take much more time out for humor than we do for sex or for eating. We wisecrack, like we breathe – all the time.

But to the research and study of humor far less attention has been devoted than to books about cooking, cocktails, or sexual finesse. Quantity, however, is compensated by quality. Practically all of the major philosophers of the past have studied the nature of humor. Countless hours have been devoted to deciphering the mysteries of laugher. But the riddle has remained a riddle. In thousands of years, merely the surface of the solution has been skimmed; the full answer elusive. The mechanism of the funny is as veiled to us as it was to our ancestors.

It is entirely possible that the resolution is contained in the present work.

Many years ago the author came to a startling and simple solution. He understood why one situation or phrase made our mouths curve upward in a smile or provoked wild laughter, whereas another situation composed of the same events and carrying the same information left us disinterested and uninvolved. The author analyzed the existing classification systems of humor as well as countless jokes, anecdotes, humoresques, comical narratives, caricatures, etc. He came upon the logic of the funny, and came to the conclusion that a quantitative evaluation is possible.

But the author in his younger years was not skilled in science and its methodology. He could not lay out his thoughts in an accessible and convincing manner. He was unable to convince the professionals. He was not then, and, for that matter, is not now an expert in human psychology or linguistics. He was constantly held back by the fear that his discovery was not at the least bit novel, that it had already been widely discussed, and worse, put aside.

Since then, forty years have gone by. In that time, the author's ideas have had time to settle and become covered with noble patina; two doctor's dissertations were defended; experience was gained in articulation of thoughts. On many occasions since, the author has had to proffer and defend enterprising technical positions.

In the course of nearly forty years the author has tested his theory with practice, and compared his formula against every joke, anecdote, and funny phrase that he encountered. All, whether written in prose or verse, fit the theory. Never had the author been forced to take the role of Procrustes, contorting situations to fit his brainchild.

At the same time, the author has punctiliously tracked the achievements of scientific progress, trying to spot the moment when someone else would arrive at the same conclusions. But this has never occurred.

Taking into consideration that the author might not have the next forty years at his disposal, he made the decision to make his theory public.

This theory may bring criticism and disparagement on the part of the reader. The author himself sees its certain failings and inevitable subjectivity. However, the theory has its strong sides, which will prove of interest to the curious reader.

The reader will be offered a concept based on the same principles as the widely accepted scientific theories. These principles are verifiability, objectivity, and quantitative appraisal. The suggested theory does not factually contradict any of the existing theories of humor, and is instead based on them, unites them, makes peace among them.

The task at hand might be considered completed if after reading this work the reader will exclaim: **"Why, everyone knows that! There's nothing new in this theory!"**

And that will be considered the highest affirmation.

HISTORICAL BACKGROUND

Chapter One

Historical Background

W hen man began to preserve the written language, the methods of transcription were prohibitively expensive. Our ancestors imprinted only the most important events in their lives on sheaves of papyrus, clay tablets, or cliff-wall petroglyphs. We would expect that such an insignificant subject matter as humor would remain outside the set of ancient records that have reached us today. (However, such a lack of records would not lead us to the conclusion that the funny was foreign to our ancestors).

Surprisingly, such records have remained, and the oldest of these can be traced back to the times of the Egyptian pharaohs. In the opinion of the renowned British investigator **Carol Andrews**, ancient Egyptian humor was not unlike the contemporary. Like us, the ancient Egyptians liked obscene jokes; they had political satire, parodies, something akin to animated cartoons, and even black humor.

Plato (427-348 B.C.) is considered to be the first great philosopher that devoted significant effort to the study of humor. The founder of philosophy did not bypass this non-serious subject. And his opinion on the subject proved to be negative. Plato saw nothing good in humor. In the treatise *The Republic* Plato examined the negative consequences of psychopathic laughter. In *Philebus*, only defects are ascribed to the comical figure. Those prone to laughter think themselves richer, handsomer, and smarter than they are in reality. **Plato considers humor a negative phenomenon, because this emotion is based on malevolence and envy, in particular laughter caused by the hardship or ill-fortune of another, or mockery of someone of lower status or privilege.** Plato did not make an attempt at the explanation of the nature of humor, but came to the considerably important conclusion that laughter can have serious consequences, including affecting the status of an entire republic.

As such, laughter was denounced by Plato. Was he wrong in his appraisal? Not so; the reader will soon understand that he was quite correct.

Many thinkers and writers arrived at the same conclusion. For instance, **Evgeny Zamyatin** in his dystopian novel *We* wrote: *"Laughter is the most frightening weapon: laughter can destroy anything, even murder."*

Indeed, laughter, pamphlets, caricatures, entire literary works were used in political battles, and often with crushing power.

There are many political regimes in which ridiculing the government is the loyal subjects' national pastime. The risks associated with the realization of this pastime rarely stop anyone. Several analysts have come to hold the opinion that an anecdote becomes interesting only when its telling can land you in jail.

Aristotle (384-322 BC) in *Rhetoric* views jokes as a form of educated snobbery. He pointed out two main features of the comic: *"The ridiculous may be defined as a mistake or deformity not productive of pain or harm to others."* It will be shown

2

below that the great philosopher was only half-right: specifically, he was right about the first half.

Aristotle was the first to introduce the concept of the effect of sudden or triggered laughter. This idea was firmly forgotten by his descendants, and became re-developed over two thousand years later in the works of Kant and Schopenhauer. In contrast to Plato, Aristotle allowed that humor, in limited quantities, could be beneficial.

Quintilian dedicated a massive composition to the study of humor; also **hypothesizing that humor contains a certain medley of truth and lies.**

The Middle Ages were not happy times for studying such a merry phenomenon as humor. The next period of active investigations into the matter coincided with the early Renaissance.

Thomas Hobbes (1588-1679) developed the views of Plato and Aristotle that **laughter has bearing on one's social status and superiority over one's peers.** In *Leviathan,* Hobbes writes that the **human race is in a constant power struggle**, and that it should not be surprising that victory goes to the one who laughs. Hobbes expressed a fruitful idea that **laughter is an expression of sudden triumph, caused by a no less sudden feeling of superiority over others or over one's past.**

Immanuel Kant (1724-1804) in *Critique of Pure Reason* asserted that *"laughter is an emotion which is born from the sudden change of an anxious expectation into nothing"* (that is, with the statement of the key word, the 'salt' of the anecdote, our predictions about the expected conclusions are unfulfilled).

For instance, the tale of a man whose hair is said to have turned grey in a single night from excess of grief won't call forth laughter, even if we don't believe the story (transition to the opposite). On the other hand, we laugh at the story of a man grieved to such an extent that his wig turns grey (transition into nothing). A good joke must contain in itself *something* that we initially take to be true, momentarily deceiving us, and the next moment vanish into nothing. This is the mechanism that provokes laughter, Kant postulated. He dissected the psychological situation brought about by the taking in of witticisms. Of course, Kant never did define the term *'something'*.

From the provided examples one could conclude that the Kantian *something* is a regular absurdity. But not every absurdity is funny and keen. To produce laughter the absurdity must be presented in a certain way, which Kant incisively delineated. He was the first to note that only a certain structure of a thought ("play of ideas") can produce laughter.

In the second half of the nineteenth century, **Herbert Spencer** again turned to analyzing the structure of laughter-causing situations. According to Spencer, laughter can be caused by a range of feelings, not always pleasant (sardonic and hysterical laughter). Strong emotional upheavals lead to a build-up of nervous energy. This energy seeks to escape, and most easily does so through those muscles which, because of low mass, have the least inertia: the mouth muscles, the mimetic muscles, the vocal apparatus, and the respiratory musculature. If those channels prove to be insufficient for the release of nervous energy, other escape channels are used, and the entire body begins to shake in convulsions. This is the mechanism of laughter, triggered by simple emotions. Spencer has a different explanation for laughter as a response to the comical. The comical inexorably signifies some sort of incongruity, but this incongruity must carry a descending character. In other words, in a comical situation we expect something big, and find something small. This is what is called a *descending incongruity*. In the opposite case, if instead of something small we suddenly discover something large, we get a feeling of *ascending* incongruity.

Arthur Schopenhauer (1788-1860) developed this idea into the so-called *"theory of the absurd"*. According to Schopenhauer, laughter appears from the recognition of incongruity between the physical expectation and the abstract conception of certain things, people, or actions; a concept that descends from Aristotle. **Success in recognition of the absurd, recognition of non-correspondence between a concept and the real thing is, according to Schopenhauer, the reason for laughter.**

This idea, as we will see, is quite close to the theory proposed in the present study, but it is not capable of explaining the most important thing: why absurdity is not always funny; what differentiates funny absurdity from the unfunny one. Although Schopenhauer tried for a complete solution to the problem of the funny and the flat, his traction, as well as his explanation of the phenomenon of the humorous, provided in a paragraph of The World as Will and Representation (1819), leaves much unexplained.

Sigmund Freud and his followers contributed significantly to the analysis of humor. In his *Jokes and Their Relation to the Unconscious* (1905) Freud, having studied most of the accessible to him works about laughter gave a psychological evaluation of wit. He arrived at the following conclusion: *"The pleasure of wit originated from an economy of expenditure in inhibition, or the comic from an economy of expenditure in thought, and of humor from an economy of expenditure in feeling."* We won't concern ourselves with picking apart the work of Freud, as he has had enough critics without us. Freud had always suffered from an oversimplified appraisal of his work. According to Freud: *"Humor is a means of obtaining pleasure despite the distressing affects which interfere with it; it acts as a substitute for the generation of these affects, it puts itself in their place. If we are in a situation which tempts us to release painful affects according to our habits, and motives then urge us to suppress these affects in statu nascendi, we have the conditions for humor. In the cases just cited, the person affected by misfortune, pain, etc., could obtain humorous pleasure while the disinterested party laughs over the comic pleasure. We can only say that the pleasure of humor results at the cost of this discontinued release of affect; it originates through the economized expenditure of affect."*

Freud's ideas found a number of followers. **D. Flagel** in the *Dictionary of Social Psychology* (in the article *"Humor and Laughter"*) moved the emphasis to the significance of cultural traditions and status of social groups. The release of energy related to humor and laughter was likewise related to the breaking down of social taboos. A similar point of view was upheld by **M. Choicie** (*"Fear of Laughter"*), construing laugher as a defense mechanism against taboos. According to him, humans, with the assistance of laugher, overcome fear of their father, mother, the government, sexuality, aggression, and so on. In this way, laugher is equal in its social importance to the arts, neuroses, and alcoholism. **E. Kris** (*"Ego Development and the Comic"*) supposed laughter to be not merely a method of release of energy, but also a return to childhood experience.

D. Levine, followed by **R. Coser** extended this thesis to social behavior as a whole, asserting that **humor and laughter always contain certain aggressiveness, regardless of whether they are directed towards a specific object.** On the contrary, **M. Eastman** (*Wit and Absurdity: Freud's Mistake*) postulated that there is such a form of humor as a nonsensical joke. Nor does folk humor, in his opinion, completely fit under the aggressive heading. The so-called children's anecdote, according to Eastman, thwarts the aggressiveness theory entirely. Eastman conjectured that humor, along with having sexual and aggressive origins, might simply be man's desire to escape an unpleasant reality.

Ludovici, like Plato, found something **"sinister" in the nature of humor.** *"There is not a single joke contained within the New Testament,"* he wrote. *"... laughter in the Bible nearly always signifies contempt, and not merriment"* (outside of isolated exceptions in the Books of Psalms and Jove).

A more serious adherent to the idea of the **aggressive nature of humor** was **Albert Rapp** (*"The Origin of Wit and Humor"*, New York: Dutton, 1951).

Henri Bergson (1859-1941) in his *"Laughter: an Essay on the Meaning of the Comic"* made a significant contribution to the examination of the social meaning of laughter. In contrast to Plato, Bergson defines the main function of laugher as the improvement of society. According to Bergson, **laugher loses all meaning outside of the social group.** This view is held by nearly all of the present-day scholars. Bergson adds that **laughter is connected to humans or to something that can in turn be connected to humans.** *"A landscape,"* writes Bergson, echoing the earlier-stated thought of **N. G. Chernishevsky,** *"may be beautiful, inviting, magnificent, drab, or repulsive; but it is never funny."* Bergson asserts that the **lone man never laughs.**

Bergson used as a springboard the conclusions of **Théophile Gautier,** who said that the comic in its most extreme form was the logic of the absurd. He came to the conclusion that *"More than one philosophy of laughter revolves round a like idea. Every comic effect, it is said, implies contradiction in some of its aspects. What makes us laugh is alleged to be the absurd realized in concrete shape, a "palpable absurdity";-- or, again, an apparent absurdity, which we swallow for the moment only to rectify it immediately afterwards;--or, better still, something absurd from one point of view though capable of a natural explanation from another, etc."*

Bergson thought that *"all these theories may contain some portion of the truth; but, in the first place, they apply only to certain rather obvious comic effects, and then, even where they do apply, they evidently take no account of the characteristic element of the laughable, that is, the particular kind of absurdity the comic contains when it does contain something absurd is an immediate proof of this desired? You have only to choose one of these definitions and make up effects in accordance with the formula: twice out of every three times there will be nothing laughable in the effect obtained. So we see that absurdity, when met with in the comic, is not absurdity in general. It is an absurdity of a definite kind. It does not create the comic; rather, we might say that the comic infuses into it its own particular essence. It is not a cause, but an effect--an effect of a very special kind, which reflects the special nature of its cause. Now, this cause is known to us; consequently we shall have no trouble in understanding the nature of the effect."*

But despite the promised absence of trouble in understanding the nature of the effect, neither Bergson nor any of the researchers that succeeded him were able to name it. They brought us closer to solving the riddle, but they did not find the answer.

Robert R. Provine, the author of *"Laughter: A Scientific Investigation."* (2001), conducted an experimental evaluation of Bergson's positions on the social nature of humor. He asked 72 students to keep a laughter journal, that is, to record when they laughed and whether they were laughing alone or in a social context. It turned out that students laughed more frequently in a social contest considerably more frequently: by approximately 30 times. Provine, like Bergson, came to the conclusion that **laughter in solitude without an audience practically doesn't exist.**

The Hungarian scholar **Arthur Koestler** in *"The Act of Creation"* and **John Morreall** contested Bergson's view about the social role of laughter: *"If I found a bowling ball in the refrigerator, this absurd situation might seem funny, even though I don't think of the bowling ball as a person."* Koestler postulated that laugher is an action without any particular purpose, entirely disconnected from the battle for survival. Laughter is a unique (luxurious!) reflex, having no specific biological function. This reflex plays a large role in our intellectual and physical development. Moreover, laughter plays a part in our battle for survival and in our battle with our misfortunes. Laughter, according to Koestler, creates, liberates, and renews. It frees us from the fear which binds our liberty.

Nor was the dilemma of humor bypassed by the author of one of the most controversial theories of the nineteenth century: **Charles Darwin.** In *"Expression of the Emotions in Man and Animal"* he expressed his views on the role and meaning of laugher as a reaction of the adaptation of organisms to the surroundings, and the evolution of laughter. Darwin thoroughly investigated the anatomy of the human and ape facial muscles, and analyzed the sounds of laugher. In most representatives of the animal kingdom, vocal signals are used to attract the opposite sex. Animals vocalize joy upon seeing their offspring, their friends, or their herd. Sounds of pleasure greatly differ from expression of horror. Wails of misfortune are characterized by a long sustained exhale and short inhale, while laughter is the opposite – a long uninterrupted inhale, and choppy short exhales.

The role of mimetic components in laughter, particularly the pulling apart of the lips consists of enlarging the resonating cavity of the mouth, which ensures a sufficient strength of the auditory signal. There is a whole series of gradations of laughter – from a barely noticeable smile, to homeric roaring. The smile is the first stage in the building of a laugh. Darwin explains in the following way: the habit of uttering sounds from a sense of pleasure first led to the retraction of the corners of the mouth and of the upper lip, and to the contraction of the orbicular muscles; and now, through association and long-continued habit, the same muscles are brought into slight play whenever any cause excites in us a feeling which, if stronger, would have led to laughter; and the result is a smile. Thus a smile turned into an independent expression of pleasure – in all the world's cultures.

John Locke in his *"Essay Concerning Human Understanding"* attempted to draw the distinction between a clever statement and a simple remark. Cleverness, according to Locke, lies first and foremost in the rapprochement of ideas and in their unity, fast and diverse, which gives the sensation of pleasure.

J. Edison, refining Locke's ideas, noted that not every union of ideas is clever, merely the unexpected unions. Moreover, **the foundation of a joke can be not only the closeness of ideas, but also an incongruity.**

Georg Wilhelm Friedrich Hegel (1770-1831) expressed

his ideas on wit in his *"Science of Logic"*. Hegel approached the analysis of wit as a form of thought. Even though it does not express the notion of things and their relationships and has for its material and content only the determinations of ordinary thinking, [wit] does bring these into a relation that contains their contradiction and *allows their notion to show or shine through the contradiction.*

In this way, the *"shining contradiction"* between reality and appearance is that thing which is common to all wit. But we can hardly accept that with this formula Hegel made plain the entire nature of wit. The phrase *"shining contradiction"* is itself in need of explanation.

Michael Bakhtin proposed his interpretation of laughter and folk culture. In *"The Work of Francois Rabelais and the Folk Culture of the Middle Ages and Renaissance"* he assumes a significant reconstruction of our artistic and ideological consciousness. In Bakhtin we find a cultural explanation of the little-studied tradition of folk humor and forms of laughter in various spheres of human creation.

While the Egyptians built pyramids and the Greeks created theater, folk culture invented the carnival. Carnival and festive laughter play an important-most role in the history of the comic. The canonical medieval culture is characterized by exclusively serious overtones. Seriousness was considered to be the only method of expressing truth and other important and useful things. Laughter, however, is just as universal as solemnity, according to Bakhtin. Laughter contains the history of society and conception of the world.

In the Renaissance epoch, laughter became an expression of the new, free, critical and historical aspect of the period. Laughter always conquered fear. The Renaissance created a new set of morals. Already with medieval humor there was the presentiment: victory over fear will come. Through laughter Man resisted fear. But in the Middle Ages, only the external fear was subdued. The Renaissance, wrote Bakhtin, overcame the internal fear.

Humor Theory

The Russian reader is well-acquainted with **Alexander Luk**'s book *On the Sense of Humor and Wit,* 1977. For many years, practically no work of a Russian scholar studying the nature of laughter was published without mention of his substantial work. Luk was the first author of the Soviet period who did the work of systemizing the theories of the funny and drew a set of deep, independent conclusions. To him belongs the original system of classification of methods that call forth laughter.

Known are the writings of **A. Dmitriev** *(Sociology of Humor: Descriptions, 1996)*, **A. Arkhipova** *(Anecdote and its prototype: the Genesis of the Text and Constraining of Genre, 2003,)* **E.** and **A. Shmelev** *(Phonetic Knowledge in the Russian Anecdote)*, located in the web of research of **M. Voinarovsky.**

Y. Borev *("On the Comic" Culture, 1962)*, **V. Frolov** *On Soviet Comedy" Culture, 1954)*, **B. Minchin** *("Priests of Feeding the Theory of the Comic", Kiev, 1959)*, **Y. Elseberg** *(Problems in the History of Sattire," 1957)*, **V.I. Karasik** *(Anecdote as Subject of Linguistic Study)*.

We direct lovers of clever Russian wordplay to the voluminous text of **Vladimir Sannikov** *"The Russian Linguistic Joke: From Pushkin to Present Day,"* Moscow, 2003. A part of that book is reserved for the analysis of puns.

The works of **L. Karassev** appeared in the late 1980s - early 1990s in Russian, French, and Polish editions. These works offered a new conception of humor and laugher. The big idea was of laughter as a cultural-historical-ontological phenomenon, which revealed its meaning when juxtaposed with its surrounding symbols. A. Dmitriev thought that Karassev's conception could be termed as "semantic", since the basis of all of the author's constructions was the hypothesis of laugher as a symbolic whole, developing according to its own internal laws.

The author relegates the conception of laughter to a realm outside of the boundaries of that which we would call "scientific knowledge." We are unable to say anything about the origin of laughter, as we have no reliable knowledge about it or any of its components, which compose the quintessence of human activity and sensuality – language, thought, ritual, mythology, and so forth. For this very reason the problem of the origin of laughter cannot be examined separately in an isolated manner. Laughter appears simultaneously with language and thought. As for the dynamics of this process, L. Karassev holds the position that **laughter appears immediately; at the same moment as all of the other important-most elements of human culture** (many linguists hold the same view). Laughter appears as a single whole, as a prevailing quality, and only then does it begin to develop, become enriched, etc.

According to Karassev, the various apparent manifestations of humor can be grouped into two types. The first type of laughter has to do with situations in which a person expresses happiness, bodily joy, "physical" or "vital" enthusiasm. Karassev calls this type the "laughter of the body," and groups it along with states which are characteristic not only of humans, but also of animals, who also are familiar with the joy of playing games and of physical delight.

The second type is associated with an evaluation of the comicality of a situation. This type of laughter can include elements of the previous type; however, its essence is that it embodies a union of emotion and reflection. This type of laughter is called the "laughter of the mind."

If the first type, the "laughter of the body", is at the bottom of human sensuality, then this "laughter of the mind" is at the top. This realm of reflection, paradoxical evaluation, is the birthplace of wit. "*In short,*" says Karassev, "*it could be said that there are two ways to laugh, and one way to cry.*"

The "laughter of the mind" is that very laughter that Aristotle was talking about when he wrote about the ability to laugh as a particular feature of humans that separated them from animals.

These last works, perhaps, comprise everything that were written in Russian.

Humor Theory

English-language literature is considerably more prolific, and the author admits that he was able to become acquainted with a large part, if not most of it, through the survey work of other authors.

Laughter is a much more accessible subject for study than the subjects studied by other sciences (in particular the natural sciences). It is always with us, and doesn't cost a penny. Nonetheless, practical studies of humor started only about a hundred years ago. Not only philosophers, but sociologists, psychologists, linguists, and professional comedians: writers, artists, and journalists started to study the question of laughter.

G. Stanley Hall, the founder of American psychology, took part in composing a questionnaire for the study of ticklishness in 1897. Perhaps he used the well-known definition of a ticking as a way of getting laughter manually. Other various studies include: **Martin's** introspective analysis (1905), the memory of funny situations (**Heim**, 1936), the stimuli that cause laughter (**Cambouropoulos**, 1930), children's laughter (**Kenderlin**, 1931, **Ding** and **Jersild**, 1932), and the study of the development of the funny (**Washburn**, 1924, **Wilson** 1931).

The intensity of research increased in the seventies and eighties of last century when international conferences on humor were organized, the first of which took place in Cardiff, Wales, 1976; and when books were published, summarizing and drawing conclusions on previous studies. Numerous periodicals are currently being published, including the International Journal of Humor Research.

Victor Raskin, currently of Purdue University, suggested the so-called semantic theory of humor (Victor Raskin, *Semantic Mechanisms of Humor - Dordrecht: Reidel, 1985*), developed alongside **Salvatore Attardo**'s (*Linguistic Theories of Humor. 1994*). The books of these authors are published in a limited print run, and are not available on the web. We were able to become acquainted with these books through the courtesy of the authors.

"The goal of the linguistic theory of humor, as formulated by its author, *was the determination of conditions sufficient and necessary for the text to be funny."*

According to the ideas of these authors (initially presented by Arthur Koestler in *"Act of Creation"*), the humoristic effect appears at the sudden juxtaposition in the mind of two unrelated contexts at the point of biosociation: *"Biosociation - a circumstance of intersection in the mind of two disjointed but logically justified associative contexts."* We laugh when two contexts, completely disparate from one another, begin to seem connected through bisociation – thus a cognitive dissonance is formed, which is compensated by the reaction of laughter. How do we recognize the comic effect? According to cognitive theories, our memory stores events in the forms of structures, which **Minsky** called frames, and Raskin and Attardo – scripts. A frame or a script is a structured description of the typical features of the object. Raskin postulates that at the foundation of the comical effect lies a collision of contexts, and not simply of semantic meaning. According to this theory, the humoristic effect arises if the following conditions are in place:

a) the text has full or partial compatibility;
b) two parts of the text are incongruous in a particular sense.

Raskin asserted that *"Any humorous text will contain an element of incongruity and an element of resolution."* The difference between Raskin's theory and the theories cited above is that Raskin gave the concept of opposition a universal semantic meaning. Later, after a discussion with Raskin, Attardo came to the conclusion that his theory falls under the category of the theories of incompatibility (see below). The result of this discussion was their collaborative work *"General Theory of Verbal Humor"* (*1991*).

Salvatore Attardo's book, and his article (*"The Linguistics of Humor"*, *2004*) comprise a reasonably exhaustive examination of the various theories of humor from the times of ancient Greek philosophers through the present. The surveyed literature includes publications from many different sources and in multiple languages. Salvatore Attardo's book and article contain a colossal amount of material, and reflect comprehensive achievements of modern scholarship in the direction of humor.

That which is not contained in the works of Attardo may be found in the writings of **Thomas C. Veatch** "*A Theory of Humor, Humor, the International Journal of Humor Research, May, 1998*", which is available on the web. It also contains an enormous amount of material, including a complete survey of everything that was ever published in the English language on the topic. It is our great pleasure to direct the reader to this source: *http://facstaff.uww.edu/shiblesw/humorbook/h8%20th eory.html*

As additional bibliographical sources, let us point out the work of **Ceccarelli** (1998) and the resource placed by him on the web:

http://www.uni-duesseldorf.de/WWW/MathNat/Ruch/research%26people.html

The number of different theories of humor at present is so extensive that agreement cannot be found even on a unified classification system. Victor Raskin believed that existing theories could be divided into three groups: incongruity theories, hostility theories, and release theories.

Incongruity theories predicate that humor appears as a **result of understanding the incongruity between the expected, and the achieved result.** This idea was proposed by Aristotle, and "discovered" several times since. The most well-known adherents of this theory are **Kant, Schopenhauer, Koestler, Paulos** (mathematical catastrophe theory), **Hazlitt, Locke, Monro, Nerhardt, Suls, Shultz**, and **McGhee**.

In recent years, **Hofstadter** and **Gabora** (1989), as well as **Coulson** (1996, 2001) advanced the cognitive blending theories. Some of the works of these authors are being prepared for publication, and so we cannot refer to them.

The theories of hostility go back to Plato, in part to Aristotle and Cicero, and find support in the works of Schopenhauer, **Hobbes**, and **Gruner** (1978, 1997). Such theories state that **funniness consists of attaining a feeling of superiority over something**, or in overcoming an obstacle, or aggression, in the attack of some object. As **Ludovici** remarked, *"in laughing, we bare our fangs."*

The theories of liberation teach us that humor is a result of the release of a type of psychic energy, liberating man from a certain amount of restraint. One of the more famous of these theories belongs to Freud. The adherents of a similar viewpoint include such authors as **Spencer** (1860), **Penjon** (1893), **Kline** (1907), **Gregory** (1924), **Eastman** (1936) and **Monro** (1951). These authors postulate that human actions are limited by numerous prohibitions – sustention of rational behavior, the need for straightforward expression of thought, and adherence to common sense. The humorous manner of expression of thought and way of socialization frees us from these restrictions; for example, through the means of the tallow jokes and anecdotes frequently cited by Freud. Subsequent studies showed that none of the mechanisms described by Freud were unique to humor. Attardo in his latest work proposes that **Freud's theory may be grouped with the theories of incongruity.**

The work of V. Raskin contains the assertion (p. 131), that all three groups of theories are well described by the linguistic theory of humor. This may be so, but does this theory give us key to answering the main question: **why do people laugh?** We did not find an answer to this question in Raskin's book.

In *"On the Comic", 1974* **B. Dziemidok** unites the conceptions of the funny into the following groups:

-- Theory of negative quality.
-- Theory of degradation.
-- Theory of contrast.

-- Theory of contradiction.
-- Theory of deflection from the norm.
-- Theories of a mixed type.

Most of the existing researches on humor are full of surface-level conjectures and contain little empirical data. These researches have a severely limited scope and completely ignore the big picture. Some of these researchers surround themselves with fancy terms, or terms they invented themselves in hope of substituting them for a true understanding of the phenomenon of laughter.

Existing empirical studies, in turn, describe valuable insights, but do not provide generalizations which make it possible to explain them.

The study of numerous works and discussions with specialists, professionally studying questions of humor, have led us to the emphatic conclusion that the mechanism of the funny is far from having being understood. A theory of humor, fully, logically, and convincingly revealing its nature, does not as of yet exist.

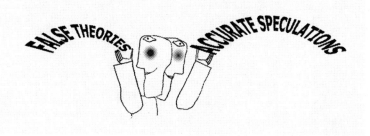

"Humor is a pervasive feature of human life...yet its nature is elusive."
(LaFollett & Shanks)

"The sacred secret of laughter... lies beyond the horizon of contemporary science."
(A. Luk)

"Humor is one of the elements of genius"
(Goethe)

"That which is shallow in the serious form may be deep in the witty."
(G. C. Lichtenberg)

Chapter Two

False Theories and Accurate Speculations

The reader should not assume that no understanding has been attained about the nature of humor. On the contrary, upon reading the available studies, it is hard to not be surprised at how closely our predecessors came to solving the eternal riddle, and how thin, at times, was a barrier separated them from the truth. It is as though the Creator offered them hints, but for some reason, these hints were neither heard nor understood.

The many scholars did so much and came so close to the solution that we have only to tie together the accurate assertions of our predecessors into a unified whole. As soon as we accomplish this, many people will exclaim: "but that's obvious!" Precisely that is the goal of the present study.

An accurate appraisal of the accomplishments is possible only in the case that a satisfactory theory is already known. We will try to give a brief summary of those theories and guesses which from the point of view of the proposed theory are either false or true. Doing this is further important in order to distinguish those theories from new material contributed by this work.

2.1. False Theories

Researchers of all times are united by one a common property. Humor researchers have investigated humor and its manifestations exactly like scientists investigate natural phenomena: that is, as a phenomenon existing independently of the researcher. Nobody grew laughter in a test tube, like homunculus. It is quite obvious that laughter exists independently of our will. Most likely, it was inherent in humanity from the moment of its appearance, instead of later forming along with civilization. Moreover, according to a number of observers, humor is also found in animals; in fact, certain characteristics of the humor of animals and of humans have unquestionable similarity.

Naturally, as a basis of the scientific conception of humor it must be accepted that humor is one of the basic forms of human activities. From here the logical conclusion is drawn that humor is one of the most primitive forms of these activities.

Therefore, we will treat A. Luk's assertion that "*the sense of humor is vaster than any definition because it is a very complex state of the soul*" as an incorrect one.

Luk's assertion that "*these qualities* (wit and humor) *do not play a decisive role in biological evolution and the battle for survival*" also seems incorrect. Luk thinks that "*having discovered these qualities in himself, Man began to cultivate and develop them. In modern society, wit and a sense of humor are quite highly valued.*"

Koestler held a similar (false, from our point of view) position, claiming that laughter is an activity without any particular useful goal, having nothing to do with the battle for survival, a *luxurious reflex*, not playing any specific biological part.

Luk agrees that humor can be defined as "*benign lampoonery*". We, however, following **Thomas Hobbes**, suppose that humor is always aimed at gaining supremacy over those around us.

We will also allow ourselves to group **Mark Eastman**'s position about the existence of innocent, meaningless jokes, and that humor (aside from sexual and aggressive causes) might be the simple desire of man to escape from an unpleasant-to-him reality, with the set of false theories.

Sigmund Freud's theory is deep and elegant. But it was not confirmed experimentally, and its role in the understanding of humor is unclear. Though many of Freud's findings were quite valuable, and were developed by his followers, including in this work.

With the false theories we will group the views of **M. Choicie**, who considered laughter a defensive reaction against the fear of breaking social taboos.

Laughter and humor, most scholars think, play an entirely different function in the development of humanity as a whole.

2.2 Accurate Speculations

Here we will cite those theories and views which, combined in a logical manner, will lead us to the elucidation of the age-old riddle. We took a liberty to label as "accurate" not those guesses which support our theory, but only those which have found wide acknowledgement and are confirmed by experimental data. For convenience's sake, we will break them up into groups.

2.2.1 The Innateness of Humor as a Psychological Phenomenon

Laughter is inherent in not only adult representatives of the human race, but also in children. **Pliny** remarked that a smile appears on an infant's face within the first few weeks of life. A baby's laughter can be caused by brightly colored objects, food, musical sounds, his mother's face, being tossed in the air by parents or close ones, a new non-frightening situation, tickling, or gentle caressing. By the end of the third month, infants start to smile not only due to unconditional stimuli, but also at their signifying conditionals. Thus, the initial biological purpose of the smile and laughter is purely informational: to inform the parents that their offspring is sated and content.

Humor itself starts to appear in children starting at a very young age. An experimental behavioral study of children in Belgium, the United States, and Hong Kong showed that boys attempt to cause laughter more frequently than girls; moreover this tendency starts at the age of 6, which many consider to be the age that humor appears.

Dmitriev studied the humor in children, beginning with the preschool age. He came to the conclusion "about the existence in children of a sort of socio-spiritual need, which no other cultural education could satisfy. When a child turns to a peer, offering to tell a joke, this is not merely a silly way of spend time, but something much greater: the exchange of valuable information about "adult" life." He postulated that children's humor "is a powerful source of forming certain political (sic!) orientation and modeling a future world view."

For preschool children, humor and jokes are not concentrated in the narrow field of their childish understanding, as an uninformed investigator might have supposed. Instead, paradoxically, 90% of anecdotes heard and recorded in preschool and kindergartens have to do with politics and the world.

Dmitriev tried to determine the proportion of children for whom humor was an important way of socializing. He discovered that *"no more than 10% of children were able to immediately upon request tell a political anecdote. But if the child knew such anecdotes, then he would compulsorily tell not one or two, but three, four, or even more. In the telling of such anecdotes, the child can demonstrate the maturity of his intellectual skills in front of his parents or friends."*

We will be daring enough to assume that Dmitriev was unable to duly access the importance of his discovery: specifically of the connection between the tendency of children to "humorize", and the tendency to advance in society. There is a large number of studies showing that not all people are predisposed towards leadership. The proportion of those who display leadership qualities is about 14%, i.e. $1/7^{th}$ of the entire population. This correlates well with the 10% found by Dmitriev, if we take into consideration the limited extent of his studies.

In countries with a developed system of democracy, that is, in those where people have the opportunity to fully develop their potential, an enormous quantity of enterprises, large and small, come to existence. Some of these enterprises consist of tens or hundreds of thousands of employees, some only of one or two. But if we conduct a statistical analysis, we find that the average number of people involved in an enterprise is around... seven. Could this be another piece of evidence that $1/7^{th}$ of the population want to be and under certain circumstances become leaders, whereas the other $6/7^{th}$ readily take up subordinate positions under these leaders?

Let us assume that this hierarchy developed not in the epoch of the democratic free market, but has existed throughout all time. We do not have universal data to back up this view, but we do have certain supporting observations. At one time, the author spent many hours in a certain establishment closed to the public - the Smolensk Historical Archive - trying to find written sources for compiling his genealogy. Thousands of works went through his hands. These were ancient handwritten notebooks, containing writings of nobles who lived in Smolensk over the course of several centuries. A part of these writings bore traces of floods, mice, and bookworms. Our ancestors' handwriting was awful, and their orthography would have caused a second-year summer school student to swell with pride. The author, whose conscience was poisoned by prime Marxist-Leninist theory, mentally prepared himself to encounter inventories of nobles' estates containing thousands, or at least hundreds of disenfranchised serfs. To his deepest surprise, he did not find more than one or two such estates. On the contrary, the number of landowners with several, sometimes one or two serfs was the predominant number. But the average amount of landowners (leaders) and serfs (subordinates) was at that same mystical level, with an approximate ratio of one to six.

We offer the reader the opportunity to conduct a survey of his circle of friends and acquaintances, and to determine what percentage of them ascribe themselves to the set of inveterate jokers, wags, and the lives of the party. Might this percentage also correlate with the ratio of natural leaders, with that same magical proportion of $1/7^{th}$?

But could humor be a primitive enough phenomenon such that it may be found not only in children, but also in animals? In addition to the above-cited observations by Darwin of primates, we refer to the experimental results of Meyer, who conducted experiments on monkeys, trying to determine which objects his subjects prefer to observe for extended periods of time. Meyer came to the conclusion that elements of aesthetical enjoyment were inherent in primates. They preferred austere forms, limited variety; those inherent characteristics of the examined object which communicated its informational value. Indeed, without strict observance of meter and other laws of versification, even poetry may not be beautiful, was the parallel that the researcher drew.

The participants in one on-line discussion on humor came out in favor of the view that humor is inherent in other animals. One wrote: *"Of my current dogs, the eldest is unusually smart. With an undisputable sense of humor. Barrymore can always tell when he's being talked to seriously, and when he's being joked with. He is not averse to joking around himself. His favorite joke is to steal a woman's slipper and toss it up and down in the air with his teeth, grinning and watching the people's reaction over his shoulder. **In the absence of an audience, slippers do not interest him.**"* Let us remember this phrase.

It appears that the given data points in favor of the theory that humor is an innate quality and can be found not only in people but in other thinking beings. If this is the case, then humor carries in itself some sort of function necessary for the survival and development of the race. This function, of course, is not comprised of mere entertainment, but must be no less important than food or sex.

But is humor primitive, or, despite its instinctive origins, is it one of the higher expressions of human reason? If the pleasure from humor is obtained as a result of the satisfaction of primitive necessities, can we suppose that for truly wise individuals, those close to the apexes of reason, this pleasure deprecates? We cannot say this for certain, but we note that there is not a single smiling icon. And there is not a single piece of evidence that Jesus laughed.

2.2.2. The Aggressive Nature of Humor

"It seems surprising that people laugh at the misfortune of others. For instance, a man is walking down a winter street, slips, wildly flails his arms, and finally falls. The reaction of the spectators is varied, but after the victim stands up and sheepishly brushes the snow off his clothes, the majority of the on-lookers smiles or laughs – the incident turned out to not be serious. The fall itself turned into a comical event, breaking the monotony of the rhythm of everyday life."

With this example, Dmitriev supposes that *"the spectator relaxes (nothing grievous or dangerous has happened!) and begins to laugh."* But is this the cause of laughter? Is empathy the reason that we obtain pleasure from the described adventure?

We pose a simple question: what sorts of things are funny, anyway? We will try to give the following definition: **an event is termed funny if it causes laughter.** Most readers will agree with this definition until the following question is posed: can we term those situations funny in which the person laughs at the misfortune of others? To our great chagrin, we must admit that such situations exist. Experimental data (**Robert R. Provine.** *Laughter: A Scientific Investigation,* p. 20) shows that *"we laugh more when bad things happen to obnoxious than to pleasant people."* According to the author, this is a point in evidence (not opinion; evidence) of the **aggressive roots of humor.**

The authors of multiple studies, writers, and historians report to us that *"in the past, the lame, the invalids, the mentally disabled, and courtiers were degraded and even killed with accompanying ridicule and laughter."*

Public executions of criminals resembled present-day festivities. The public laughed and caroused as at a show, food and drinks were distributed among the crowd, and jesters and fools entertained the public, causing an even greater rejoicing.

And that's nothing! When Jesus was dying on the cross, many among the crowd found this amusing, and exchanged jokes. They found it funny.

But have such times passed? Are there no people in present times who laugh, seeing a physical deficiency in a neighbor, or who roll with laughter when someone slips on the ice or runs after a hat blown around by the wind (in such a case, even the most polite person might have a hard time holding back a smile).

And not just this. Unfortunately, even today the news inform us that mob violence, including mass-murders all around the world is accompanied by... laughter.

In 1999, crowds of people laughed during the ethnic genocide in Indonesia and Kosovo. In 1999 in Littleton, Colorado, two criminals shot masses of people. Some witnesses of the event remained. Aaron Cohn, a survivor of the massacre, later told some reporters that both of the murderers *"laughed. They were just hooting and hollering. They were having the time of their life."* (*"Death Goes to School with Cold, Evil Laugher",* Denver Rocky Mountain News, 21 April, 1999).

And don't most of us experience intense euphoria when a well-placed joke puts our opponent in a funny, unfavorable, frequently demeaning position? Moreover, to do this it's not at all necessary to demonstrate your real mental superiority. The power of the joke is that it does not necessarily have to be well-argued. **Its purpose is to psychologically elevate the joker over his rival,** and to place the latter in a foolish position. An important and irrefutable observation to which we will refer many times is the fact that **the joker and his target perceive the joke,** especially a particularly offensive one, **entirely differently.** The victim, as a rule, is not up to laughing. And this once more speaks to humor being a type of a **weapon in the battle for social status.**

According to the theory of psychoanalysis, in certain situations, humor and its derivative laughter play to the aggressive behavior of groups. **S. Freud** noted that for the tendentious humor, three persons are needed: first, someone who uses laughter (wit); second, a target for aggression; and third, someone who receives the goal of laughter (wit) - the extraction of pleasure *('I' and 'It').*

Freud also supposed humor to be one of the manifestations of instincts – sexual and aggressive. According to Freud, humor is as much a means of the attraction of the female as the magnificent tail of the peacock or the bright comb of the rooster.

Unexpected confirmation of this view is offered to us by modern genetics. **Vasiliy Velkov** *("The Reason of Evolution and the Evolution of Reason", Lebed, #375, May 16 2004, in Russian)* informs us that *"sexual selection is targeted at the strengthening of secondary masculine characteristics, and at the same time, at increasing the degree of their appeal to the females. Overall, there exists a positive connection between the ability of males to convincingly demonstrate their secondary sexual characteristics and the ability of the females to appraise them and then accept their genes. The more attractive the males, the faster and more frequently they are selected by the females. And the sooner their daughters start doing the same thing, and the more attractive their sons will be. With sexual* *selection, the process of evolution speeds up. But secondary sexual characteristics can be not only morphological, but also behavioral: the capacity for leadership, for obtaining resources, etc. And behavior depends on general cognitive abilities; on the level of intellect.*

Evolutionary models in which sexual selection is based on behavioral and not morphological characteristics show that in this case evolution proceeds even more rapidly than when selection is based only on an attractive physicality.

"As for evolutionary reason for intraspecific aggression – this is that same mechanism which chooses the "stronger" genes for transmission to future generations. Genetic programs of aggression always act simultaneously with the genetic programs that control aggression, so that the entire population isn't destroyed. The evolutionary path of the species - reproduction, slow degeneration, or rapid self-destruction - will depend on the degree of balance between these oppositely directed genetic programs.

*There are two main complimentary theories of evolution of the intellectual abilities of Homo sapiens and his ancestors. One of them is based on the fact that **high intellect** (and associated advantages) undergoes a significant positive sexual selection. The other theory (the so-called "Machiavellian") is based on the idea that subpopulations not having the intellectual capacity for adequately responding to aggression undergo **strong negative natural selection**. Sexual selection towards the strengthening of the intellect is ensured because **males with a high intellect have an advantage in the transference of their genes**; as ones who hold a leadership position in the hierarchy, they have a harem or the right of the first night.*

*And the evolutionary significance of such high human qualities as **wit**, eloquence, musicality, and inventiveness is as attractive behavioral characteristics for the transfer of genes to future generations. Significantly, in the X-chromosome the genes coding for the reproductive functions are located next to the genes for intellectuality, and, as it has been recently shown,* *deficiencies in the latter change the functions of the former. Indeed, among individuals with a low IQ (lower than 70), over 30% don't leave descendants, while among those with an IQ higher than 131, only 3-4% don't have children. The evolutionary function of this location of sexual X-chromosomes is evident."*

If the given genetic data is correct, then the sense of humor is indeed linked to basic instincts. We could say that **a sense of humor is built into us like the homing instinct is built into the sperm.**

D. Levine, followed by **R. Koser** advanced Freud's thesis on social behavior as a whole, claiming that humor and laughter **always contain a certain level of aggression**, regardless of whether or not it is directed at a specific object.

Albert Rapp (*"The Origin of Wit and Humor"*, New York: Dutton, 1951) and his followers thought that *"laughter is the offspring of hatred and hostility. If hostility was not innate in mankind, laughter wouldn't exist (nor, for that matter, a need for the funny).* **All contemporary forms of wit and humor contain evidence of its aggressive origins.** *In some witticisms this comes through more clearly; in some it's disguised. But its roots are contained in every one, if only one has the desire and ability to recognize this fact. But many people simply don't express the desire.*

Ridicule, for example, bares our fangs and claws. The great majority of jokes and witticisms that reach us via radio [at the time that the book was being written, television had not yet come into use] *contain elements of ridicule. Certainly, they are subdued. Certainly, a person living in civilized society can accept them. But savagery is still concealed within."*

"This," continues Rapp, *"is one of the greatest paradoxes: even though there exists something hostile and derisive in laughter, at times some forms of the funny are full of charm and affability. A good sense of humor is one of our greatest merits. The ability to see something funny in our surroundings, to make those around us laugh, is one of our most beloved*

characteristics.

How can we explain this paradox? How can the same object be noble and low, affable and hostile, a potential blessing, and potential danger? All of the important questions posed by people about humor and laughter culminate in precisely this." The answer to these questions is given in the present investigation.

Rapp attempted to reconstruct the evolution of the funny: *"the sole source from which all of the contemporary forms of wit and humor developed is the triumphant roar in an ancient duel."* A likely outcome of such a duel was a rejoicing winner and a mournful (at best) loser. The way in which the winner released his energy was through laughter, and the unlucky wretch...cried. The party of the conqueror also laughed, and those who belonged to the camp of the conquered grieved. Rapp supposed that ridicule was the first, and for a long time, the only form of laughter. The caveman laughed at physical misfortunes of others, as they foretold of a coming victory in battle. Subsequently, intentional mockery began to supplant the battle, and probably became one of the ways in which the defeated could take revenge.

Rapp thought (and correctly so) that the tendency to rejoice, even over serious misfortunes of others is far from having been outlived.

Has it been long since the verbal battle displaced the physical? Did this happen in the cave-dwelling years, or when people began to construct cities? We think that humor developed at the moment that humanity appeared.

Battles for social leadership exist among animals as well, but animals hardly fight to the death. Sometimes their duels are limited to demonstrations of supremacy of size or aesthetics, as in peacocks. Sometimes the duel comes to head-butting or shoving.

Even venomous snakes don't bite each other. Animals have ways of morally overcoming their opponents. Why not allow that primitive humans employed "moral combat"? We think

32

that humor must have had a place in the ancient world. It was likely a part of everyday live of the cave dweller, who was no less intelligent than you or I, my respected civilized contemporaries.

In modern times, physical entanglements have turned into duels of wit. Daily we compete and sharpen our competitive mastery not in physical, but in mental superiority, wherein our wit and our **ability to find solutions** serve as weapons.

We offer two more opinions.

Martin Grotjahn (*"Beyond Laughter. New York: McGraw-Hill, 1957*) wrote: *"To summarize, wit begins with an intention to injure, which our culture causes us to repress. ... The better the disguise, the better the joke."*

William Fry (*"Sweet Madness"*, *Palo Alto, CA: Pacific Books, 1963)* went even further. Examining the relations between individuals engaged in laughter, he hypothesized that **humor contains aggression of one individual against the other**. He drew a parallel between a verbal duel and a real battle engagement. In this competition we have all the chances of losing, without even realizing the fact that we are engaged in a fight.

The importance of humor for mankind is underscored by the observation that very few people will agree that they have no sense of humor. **Steven Leacock** wrote: *"strange as it is, I have never met a person who wouldn't think the same of himself. Each admits, when he has to, that he has poor vision or that he can't swim or shoot a rifle. But God forbid you express doubt in friend or acquaintance's possession of a sense of humor – you will inflict fatal offence."* It is as though this sense is instinctively considered vital.

Darwin and **Spencer** thought that laughter plays an **important role in our survival.**

Dmitriev wrote that *"the entire system of creation and use of the sense of humor can be thought of as a unique mirror of the public essence of man; one of the forms of self-assertion."*

"Like a boulder is the weapon of the proletariat and tanks are the weapons of the government, so the anecdote (author's note - political) *is the weapon of the intelligentsia."*

Objectively, and a bit abashedly **we must admit that laughter is related to dominating others, and its aggressive nature is experimentally confirmed.**

And if the reader still has some doubt on the matter, we ask him to turn his attention to two well-known facts.

First: children are frequently cruel in their jibes. Remember your own childhood, your classroom, your street life, your summer camp. Stretch your memory.

Second: Analyze the relationships of very close people; namely, members of the same family. How many families can we find in which the husband, wife, mother-in-law, children, brothers and sisters don't compete daily for leadership, influence, and decision-making?

2.2.3. The Social Implications of Humor

The expression – "the management jokes" is well known to us. But do we realize the real implications of this short formula? Imagine a certain group of people in free association, each having a different social status. It would be false to connect this status with the intellectual potential of the people comprising this group. In it might be older people who have had the time to become professors or generals, but also gifted younger people "carrying" a marshal's baton in their haversack or graduate briefcase.

R. Provine conducted a series of interesting studies in professional collectives. Observations of one of them, consisting of psychologists, showed that the most high ranked individuals made an average 7.5 jokes each during this period; those slightly lower in the hierarchy an average of 5.5 jokes per person, and the lowest-ranked professionals only an average of 0.7 jokes.

Can we imagine a group of officers, different in rank, who

would freely exchange banter with each other? More likely, the generals' jokes would dominate this medium. And we don't think this is because the title of the general is conferred on someone for his comedic abilities. The author had had to spend some time in a military hospital, where the favorite divertissement of the ugly blue robe-clad patients was playing dominoes. The game caused great animation and drew spectators. Unlucky partners were ridiculed with military directness and roughness. One fine day, the patients became witnesses to an memorable scene. One of the more hapless and ridiculed players was checking out of the hospital and came to play a last round with his partners. He played as poorly as ever, but Lord, the desire to laugh at him completely disappeared. For before ensigns and junior officers suddenly appeared a man in the uniform of a colonel. That day, the jokes were made exclusively by him. And always successfully!

One can observe the social division of jokers and their targets to an even greater extent in countries where the caste system was preserved. In southern India, for example, the men who belong to the lowest caste servilely and foolishly giggle when speaking to a representative of a higher caste. But that same person suddenly begins to speak intelligently and clearly in the presence of individuals from a lower caste.

Indeed, what need for jokes does an absolute monarch have? We are all acquainted with such collections as "Physicists joke", "Musicians joke", but who has ever seen collections such as "Kings joke" or "Generals joke"? Presidents – those on the other hand do joke. For presidents aren't kings or generals; they are elected by the people. Candidates for presidency joke too – and how! Not a single campaign speech manages without humorous passages or sarcasm. Humor in the democratic system is a weapon in the battle for power; moreover, it is a weapon as deadly as it is irrational. When **Ronald Reagan** was getting ready for the pre-election debates, his opponent **Jimmy Carter** found a soft spot in the program of his challenger, and constructed many questions around this point.

During the decisive televised discussion. President Carter asked his question one more time. Reagan didn't even think to answer it. He looked ironically at his opponent, and uttered with a tinge of annoyance: *"Oh no, there you go again"*. And … he won the election. President Carter, who in all honesty was correct, lost.

R. Provine (p. 30) came to the unequivocal conclusion that *"humor has such high social value that only those higher on the hierarchical scale can afford it."*

The social nature of humor becomes even more evident when we answer the question: who do we laugh for? We breathe, eat and drink even when alone. We don't lose the desire to eat or drink a glass of water if there's no one standing next to us who could observe it. Do we laugh for ourselves or for the sake of others?

R. Provine asked his students to keep a special journal in which they were to keep track of when they laughed and under what circumstances. It turned out that the students laughed 30 times more frequently in the presence of others than when alone.

The author of this work conducted his own mini-study. He quizzed surrounding individuals of different ages and genders whether they were inclined to laugh in conditions of absolute solitude, that is, in their sleep. Not one of the surveyed could remember a single episode. When dreaming, we don't have an audience. Who should we laugh for?

Let us site two more interesting observations. R. Provine conducted investigations of who laughed more often: males or females, performers or the audience.

The answer to the first question proved ambiguous, as illustrated by the following table:

Humor Theory

Performer	Audience (pre-dominantly)	Episodes	Speaker laughs	Audience laughs
Male	Male	275	75.6%	60.0%
Female	Female	502	86.0%	49.9%
Male	Female	238	66.0%	71.0%
Female	Male	185	88.1%	38.9%

Notice that the men (who predominantly act as leaders) are not entirely inclined to laugh at the jokes of the opposite sex, whereas women not only laugh more frequently, but laugh more at men's jokes than at those by representatives of their own gender.

The above table gives us one additional key to understanding the nature of humor. If we limit ourselves to the study of removed theories, explaining what is funny and how the <u>resolution of a contradiction</u> leads us to laughter, we would never be able to approach an answer to the simple question: why do performers laugh more frequently than the listeners? But from the experimental data it follows that the performers laugh more willingly than the audience. Why does a person telling a joke for the thousandth time laugh more loudly and contagiously than those surrounding? At the same time, if among the listeners is another person who's heard the joke at least once before, he, as a rule, doesn't laugh. To him, it's boring.

"Any person," writes Dmitriev, *"when interacting with others, as a rule tries to maintain his image, hold up his prestige. An admission of the latter from the side of others is a need which stimulates the activeness of behavior. Doubtless, the reader knows from his own experience that a teller of anecdotes is never satisfied with the story alone. Its recognition by the crowd, if, of course, it happens, brings the raconteur incomparable satisfaction.*

Could this commonly observed fact be direct indication that **humor is aimed at the achievement of superiority over those surrounding, on heightening the social status** of the "humorist"?

Then why does the audience laugh? Could we explain its laughter as a similar aim towards increasing its social status? We will see below that this supposition is not without sense.

It's evident that not a single theory can explain the multifarious nature of humor if it doesn't take into account its social aspects. Let us take a broad genre such as parody. A skilled parody invariably calls forth a smile and is predestined for a longer lifespan than the original parodied work. Everyone knows and remembers the magnificent Alexander Ivanov and his inimitable manner of hosting the TV show *"Around Laughter"*. But how many people remember and know the names of the poets he parodied?

Let us simulate this situation. Imagine that you live in the USSR, you are a well-known, venerated poet, laureate, surrounded by family, getting ready to watch the show "Around Laughter." Recently you published a poem - beautiful, enthusiastic and full of all Soviet dignity: *"In any case, I will not kiss up to Ford!"* Suddenly from the television's screen **V. Lifschitz's** parody is broadcast across the nation:

> To Robert Rojdestvenski Ford cries aloud:
> "Why are you, Robert, so unbearably proud?
> Robert, a single hot kiss's all I crave!"
> "No, - answers Robert, - no, Mister, behave!"

> *Za Robertom Rozhdesvenskim, ridaya, mister Ford:*
> *"Ah, pochemu ti, Robert, tak nesterpimo gord?*
> *Ti podari mne, Robert, goryachit potseluy!"*
> *"No, - otvechaet Robert, - no, mister, ne baluy!"*

Your family members, especially the children and grandchildren, laugh; but is the situation funny to you? You, a famous poet, were just ridiculed in front of the entire nation.

Readers of the elder Russian generation may remember the

Humor Theory

"Twelve Chairs Club", which occupied the 16th page of the "Literaturnaya Gazette". Born of the imagination of **V. Vladin**, the great people-connoisseur and soul-lover **E. Sazonov** unrestrainedly ridiculed writers and poets in his talented parodies. The soul-lover spared no one. Not all of the parodied liked this, but matters hardly ever dissolved into protests. This went on until E. Sazonov composed a parody on the author of the multivolume book on the life of Vladimir Lenin, the live classic **Marietta Shaginian**. This wasn't the first humoristic work dedicated to this prolific novelist. In the 20s, **Alexander Archangelsky** dedicated the following quatrain to her:

> Doubt it not, her life work's ardor
> A single page will not subsist:
> Poetess, lecturer, carder,
> Sage of wool, and novelist.

> *Shirotu eyo razmaha*
> *Ne ulozhish' v pischiy list:*
> *Poetessa, lector, pryaha,*
> *Sherstoved i romanist.*

The wise A. Archangelsky knew what and to whom to write in the hard times he had to live and work. This epigram heightened the social status of the novelist. E. Sazonov, on the other hand, did not appreciate the situation. Not having our theory of humor at his behest, he published a witty parody on the prolific writer. And the writer... got offended. In a few issues, an official apology and admission of tactlessness and impropriety of the parody on Marietta Shaginian was published on the 16th page of the "LG". For some reason the evaluation of the parody by the readers of the "LG" and by the writer turned out to be diametrically opposite.

Bergson thought that *"laughter possesses healing powers. Intended for derision, it must cause moral pain to the person at whom it is directed. By means of the funny, society takes its re-*

venge on those freedoms which are accompanied by laughter. If the laughter carries a touch of sympathy or empathy towards its object of ridicule, it doesn't fulfill its mission." It was noted (**D.H. Monro**, *"Argument of Laugher. Melbourne: Melbourne University Press, 1951*) that **laughter could also play a defensive role**. We will return to this fruitful idea in Chapter 3 when we look at the defensive functions of humor.

The thesis about the social nature of humor becomes even more convincing if we pose the question of what the antithesis of funny is. If laughter is an expression of pleasure and rising up the social ladder, then what psychological state expresses an unhappy state of mind, and a descent down that same ladder?

This question was addressed by **L. Karasev**. Unlike **A. Ahiezer,** he offered as a type of antithesis to laughter the feeling of shame. This initially unexpected solution has its logic, supported by much objective material which the author gathered from many different sources, including philosophy, psychology, history, philology, and so forth.

The antithesis of laughter and shame form an ideological axis of the entire concept of Karasev's study of laughter's past, its conception, and today's and tomorrow's problems of laughter. Karasev finds all of the parameters corresponding to laughter in the phenomenon of shame. The author marks the "intellectual", reflexive character of shame, its suddenness, unpredictability of the moment of its manifestation, impossibility of its suppression through reason, even though by its nature it is fully reasonable, the strength of the affect, its connection with the realms of ethics and aesthetics, etc.

According to Karasev, **shame is laughter turned upside down**. Shame is the *"negative modus"* of laughter; their relationship can be found not only in developed forms, but in the very point of their inception. Shame, like laughter, proves to be dual: there is *"shame of the body"* and there is *"shame of the mind'*. If the *"laughter of the mind"* historically uses the premade mask of the *"laughter of the body"*, so the *"shame of the* *mind"* similarly uses the mask of its primitive predecessor - *"shame". Having appeared, shame and laughter act very similarly: both come unasked, possess us fully, stop from time to time and then start up again. It's as hard to control shame as it is a burst of laughter. Like the spasms of laughter, which return us to the wonderful moment of discovering our supremacy, "spasms" of shame return us to the situation in which our faults became apparent and recognized "inside". Moreover, in both cases a real external-physical pragmatic is absent: shame, bringing us strong and quite real sufferings, is in reality not connected with any real, actual threat. Laughter, bringing us strong joy, in no way is correlated with a real actual fortuity. Through shame, we don't become poorer, nor do we become richer through laughter."*

This wonderful comparison gives us another argument in favor of the idea that **laughter is connected with the progression upwards on the social ladder** (as opposed to shame, when we progress downward), and humor is the means for this advancement, our weapon in social interaction.

2.2.4. Laughter as an expression of pleasure

It's unlikely that we need to spend much effort to convince our readers of the validity of the position stated in this subheading. Nearly all of the investigators are united on this account. Laughter is caused by pleasure. We laugh when we feel good. But only on rare occasions does a person laugh when he just feels good. He must feel really good! Many remember the night scene from the film *"War-Time Romance"*, in which a man dressed in his underclothing sticks his head out from a third floor window and laughing shouts across the entire street: "Wooondeeeerful!!!" while his happy and embarrassed wife pushes him away from the window. We can understand this man. At that moment, he felt ve-rrry wonderful!!!

Laughter is the innate reaction to feeling good, inherent not only in man, but in the higher-order animals – monkeys, for example. The newborn begins to smile very early. Its smile and laughter are indicators of purely physical comfort, the satisfaction of his first-order aims and needs, most of all, of hunger. Smiles and laughter are natural reactions to the satisfaction of desire. In very young people, laughter serves as an indicator of the expression of health; of the excess and activity of vital forces.

With age, development, and formation of a person's social connections, laughter gains a social role, becomes one of the means of social interaction. With age, along with his first-order goals, the person develops second-order goals and their concrete expressions – wants. Their satisfaction similarly brings about positive feelings, which are externally expressed through smiles and laughter.

Dmitriev correctly assumed that *"The laughter of joy and the laughter of the mind are expressed in the same form, and this is the reason for the traditional contrasting of laughing and crying. Laughter is a sign of joy; this is why it's so natural to contrast it to tears."*

A. Luk confirmed this idea, and added that *"the greatest joy can be obtained by a person through mental exertion"*. A well-known scholar, the author of *"A History of Physics"*, Nobel Prize laureate **Max von Laue** wrote that *"understanding how the diverse and labyrinthine phenomena of mathematics are reduced to the simple and harmoniously beautiful Maxwell's equations is one of the most powerful experiences accessible to man"*.

And here is what the great naturalist Charles Darwin had to say in his autobiographical papers:

"I have discovered, though unconsciously and gradually, that the level of pleasure, brought about by...the mental effort is incomparably higher than the pleasure brought about by some technical skill or sport. My chief enjoyment ... throughout the course of my entire life had been scientific work and the exultation caused by it allowed me to forget at times, and sometimes removed entirely my perennially poor health."

As a physiological expression of pleasure, the act of laughter is pleasant in itself, causes euphoria, and a sense of well-being and comfort: *"Of all of the bodily movements, which affect both the body and soul, the laughter is the most healthy: it enhances digestion, blood flow sweating, and revitalizes the vital forces in all organs"*, writes **C.Hufeland,** the medic of the Prussian king **Friedrich** in *"Macrobiotics"*.

Here is the well-known opinion of **Sydenham**, the outstanding British physician of the XVII century: *"The arrival of a good clown into a village does more for its health than 20 asses laden with drugs"*.

A. Luk justly pointed out that laughter could be caused both by a feeling of comfort (including physical comfort), as well as suddenly thwarted danger. Luk thought that *"the act of laughter in itself is pleasing, calls forth euphoria, a feeling of well-being and comfort, being the physiological expression of pleasure"*.

But a good mood is not the only reason for laughter. We cannot laugh all the time, even if living in the best of all possible worlds. To cause laughter, it is necessary for the happy state to exceed its usual level, to make a splash, an impulse. We need the <u>amplitude of this impulse</u> to greatly exceed the level of merely a good mood.

2.2.5. Conditions for the appearance of the funny

The question implied in the heading of this section is not at the least targeted at the disclosure of the nature of the funny. To discover the reasons for the appearance of laughter and the reasons for laughter are two completely different tasks. Everyone knows that an egg dropped on the table from a height of 1 cm has chances of remaining intact, whereas an egg that falls from the table to the hard surface of the floor doesn't have those chances. But to understand the reason for this, the genius of Isaac Newton was necessary, who told us of the basic laws of mechanics.

Performing elementary experiments with magnets, even the most unprepared observer can determine that two magnets are sometimes attracted to each other, and sometimes repelled. A simple explanation for this phenomenon was found. It consisted in that one end of the magnet was termed the "north pole", and the opposite, the "south pole" and N-pole is attracted to the S-pole and repelled from the like. There was certainly practical sense in this explanation, but it got us no closer to understanding the nature of magnetic interaction than would have coloring the N-pole blue, and the S-pole red. Only much later, when it was discovered that the magnetic field of constant magnets was caused by electrons spinning in parallel planes, thus enhancing each others' magnetic fields, that our understanding widened to the level of present physical theory.

Laughter exists independently of our wishes. We have to treat it as a given, a natural phenomena. It is evident that the study of this phenomenon must begin with the study of the conditions of its conception. More precisely, with the conditions of conception of that powerful brief impulse which gives us an objective, though as of yet incomprehensible feeling of joy.

G.W.F. Hegel, in *"Science of Logic"* provided original, deep judgments on the question of interest to us. He approached the analysis of wit as a form of thought. Hegel wrote that *"the usual understanding grasps differences and contradictions, but not the transition from one to the other, whereas that's the most important."* He thought that wit carries in itself contradiction, expresses it, brings things into relation to each other, *allows their notion to show or shine through the contradiction,"* but does not express understanding of things and their relations. The thinking mind, according to Hegel, sharpens the dulled differentiating of the different, the simple variety of understandings to significant distinction, to contradiction.

In present times, it is accepted that any witty statement is based on some kind of contradiction, some unexpectedness, contradicting strict logic.

Hegel came very close to determining the nature of humor. But neither he nor his followers could penetrate the thin barrier, separating them from truth.

We can hardly say that with his verbal formula Hegel had exhausted the nature of wit. The words *"shining contradiction"*, as the following examples show, are themselves in need of decipherment.

William Hazlitt gives a long list of things that make people laugh. For example: a caricature of a person with a nose in the shape of a bottle, or the form of a midget next to a giant. We laugh at the clothing of foreigners, and they at ours. Three chimneysweeps and three Chinese men, having run into each other on a London street laugh at each other until they all collapse, and so on and so forth.

S. Freud, C. Darwin, Eastman and many others thought that to laugh, one needs to be in a happy state of mind.

Freud moreover thought that the **person must be receptive to the joke; expecting it.**

We know through experience that many comedians, even those who haven't read Freud, prepare their audience, informing it that a joke or a humorous anecdote will follow. Sometimes they use an announcement of the sort: *"that was a joke, this is how I joke."* A brilliant method was used by **Michael Zhvanetsky**. He came out on the stage and dropped a completely innocent line to the audience: *"here's what's interesting: the minister of meat and dairy industries exists and is looking well."* After which there would be a pause. And only in about 10 seconds, the Soviet audience would understand that it was a joke, and a wave of growing laughter would roll over the audience.

Freud correctly assumed that humor is better received in circumstances favorable to its reception. An experienced toastmaster only begins to joke for real after the guests had gone through several wineglasses. The "warmed up" guests are more easily stirred to a humorous spirit. The boundary is very thin. One regular joker told the author that once in his life, even this approach failed. *"See,"* he said, *"I started joking as usual after about the third glass. And I can see that it's not going well; they're not laughing. What's the matter? Then I understood: it was cold in the room; so the audience didn't get warmed up after the first three rounds".*

John Locke in his *"Essay Concerning Human Understanding"* attempted to draw the distinction between a clever statement and simple judgment. Judgment, according to Locke, consists of a thorough separation of ideas. It focuses not on similarity, but on differences, however small they might be. The purpose of judgment, Locke thought, was to avoid error based on random, trivial similarity.

Cleverness, he thought, lies first and foremost in the rapprochement of ideas and in their unity, quick and varied, which gives the sensation of pleasure.

J. Edison, refining Locke's ideas, noted that not every union of ideas is clever, merely the unexpected unions. Moreover, the foundation of a joke can be not only the closeness of ideas, but also their incongruity.

A. Luk came very close to understanding humor when he tried to analyze the role of the time factor in the reaction to the comic. He cites Mark Twain in his analysis of the importance of the pause, and comes to the conclusion that to determine the **"salt" of the joke or anecdote takes a certain amount of time.**

*"If the idea becomes immediately apparent, or if on the other hand it takes too long to figure it out, then the effect of the witticism decreases significantly, and sometimes vanishes entirely. Though the occasions in which the listeners "get" the joke several days hence and laugh aren't all that infrequent. Still, **there exists a certain optimal time for processing."***

Miroslav Voinarovsky (2003) defined humor as a *"suddenness sharply converted into understanding"*. He, like A. Luk, very nearly approached the resolution of the funny, having given attention to the time factor. Voinarovsky wrote: *"Man cannot predict ahead of time what will be said, and a* *pause happens, a delay in understanding. It is not without reason that anecdotes are set up as simple and sudden riddles: one must quickly recover from the suddenness, and then figure out what the speaker meant. The search for the answer should not take up much time. Not over 10 seconds. Otherwise the comical effect will be lost. Why this happens – <u>we can try and guess</u>* (underlined by us), *but this is a completely different question."*

It is even more important for the comprehension to happen at once, suddenly, almost instantly. If it happens gradually, like in the solution of a problem, then the humorous effect won't be there. This means that the desired solution must be very simple, not divisible into multiple steps, each of which must be solved sequentially. **The comprehension must happen quickly, not more than one, maximum 2 seconds after the person has started to figure out the solution.** Then that selfsame effect appears – like a flash, a beat of a drum or a shove, which externally discharges into laughter or a smile.

However, when we understand the meaning hidden in the anix (the "riddle"), this proves to us that we are after all smart enough. This removes the suspicion of our own stupidity. Which brings happiness. This also explains the need for the rapid comprehension. If it takes too long to guess the anix, that means we're stupid. If we solve it step by step, smoothly, then this appears as a more serious effort than the answer, which appears instantly in the moment of comprehension, required.

It is pleasant to rise over others, but even more pleasant to rise over the great. It is clear that the difficult path of ambition – to make something great – in the given case is especially difficult. There remains the easy way: through the degradation of others.

Alexander Luk thought that *"perhaps that which is common to all types of jokes is their step outside the limits of formal logic"*. In the variants of wit that he dissected: absurdity, false contrast, false strengthening, and others, this step beyond the limits of formal logic is expressed simply in the violation of the laws of identity, contradiction, excluded third, and sufficient reason. Luk arrives at a splendid guess: *"Finding and suddenly realizing the logical mistake, especially someone else's, is probably that switch that turns on positive emotion and its accompanying laughter – on the condition that there are no causes suppressing the positive emotion. Laughter in this case is an expression of the intellectual triumph of finding the error."*

This expression of A. Luk starts to uncover the veil over the mystery of the funny, but does not give an answer to the main question. If laughter is an expression of intellectual triumph, then why is even greater triumph not accompanied by peals of laughter? A person delights in having noticed a typo in a poem: *"And what rough yeast, its hour come at last, Slouches toward Bethlehem to be born"*. But why did that same person, having solved an incomparably more difficult intellectual problem, for instance a complex mathematical example, or a chess etude, or a non-trivial equation, which he really can be proud of, does he so rarely dissolve into bouts of laughter?

All of the theories of humor known to the author halt at that question. They explain that humor is caused by contradiction, which demands resolution, a solution exactly as the early theories of magnetism led to the discovery of the poles, but at the same time the mechanism remains completely veiled as in fog.

Contemporary linguistic theories are a characteristic example. All of them converge on the position of Hegel, but attempts to explain the nature of humor lead only to the examination of *"shining contradiction"* from different angles, some from the point of view of semantics, and some from semiotics and other complex objects, accessible only to specialists.

Meanwhile, **the mechanism of humor is simple and primitive**. Humor is accessible to all layers of society; moreover, it's more accessible to the lower layers to a large extent than to the higher. For this reason, the understanding of its na-

ture should also be simple. Simple and intelligible to any.
But we have not yet discovered its explanation.

2.2.6. A mathematical approach

A science can only be called thus when it is mathematically
systemized.

Naturally, the representatives of the psychological and linguistic sciences aren't always able to do this task, but attempts
at verifying hypotheses with algebra had been made. Among
others, attempts have been made in the field of humor and corresponding studies.

The brain, as we know, is capable of performing most complex mathematical and logical operations completely unconsciously. What if it performs those same operations when it's
perceiving humor? Is it possible to compose some, even approximate, mathematical equations which describe this work
and give as a result a value of the amplitude of emotions?
When this (completely individual) amplitude is exceeded,
laughter appears as a reaction. A small amplitude leads to an
internal smile, a hardly noticeable change of facial expression;
a high amplitude stretches the lips into a grin, and an even
higher one leads to the generation of audible jerky sounds
which we call laughter.

Leibniz' statement that *"music is the rejoicing of the soul,
which calculates, without knowing it itself,"* which at first
glance seems to have little to do with the matter at hand, is in
fact quite relevant and gives us a hint to what is actually happening when we perceive humor.

Birkhoff thought that aesthetic delight depends on harmonic interrelations in the system of perceived object. He even
suggested the formula

$$M = O/C$$

where M is the aesthetic measure of the object, O – the ordering, and C – the complexity. Birkhoff claimed that aesthetic pleasure could be reduced to mathematical laws of rhythm, harmony, equilibrium, and symmetry.

Morris adhered to a slightly different point of view. He thought that the perfect poetical measure is so monotonous that it becomes unbearable. This is why poets turned to free verse, to changes in rhythm. Similarly in the realm of the graphic arts: geometric proportions of the outside world are a measure from which art must always retreat. The degree of the retreat is determined not by laws, but by the artist's instinct. It is precisely this retreat from ideal laws of nature which makes a work of art beautiful. A simple peasant pot, according to Morris, contains more charm than a Grecian urn with a perfect geometric form. Morris' ideas, actually, do not contradict, but complete the views of Birkhoff. To our eyes, a person receives the most pleasure when he makes subconscious operations (calculations) which correspond to the upper limit of his abilities. From monotonous, everyday work, it's difficult to achieve the pleasure that comes with an intellectual triumph. Thus poets, supersaturated with iambic tetrameter, began to invent more difficult work for the brain; the painters left Malevich's *"Black Square"* and landscapes with birches behind, and began to search for new forms which would satisfy their heightened demands.

Humorists are likewise in search of new forms. We will show that this movement found their highest embodiment in the so-called abstract anecdotes.

Victor Raskin offered the following formula of the funny:

$$X = f(\text{Speaker, Listener, Stimulus, Life Experience,}$$
$$\text{Psychology, Situation, Society}),$$

where X can take on positive (Funny) as well as negative (Unfunny) meanings.

M. Voinarovsky gives the following formal description of the mechanism of suddenness and its resolution, which we will

Humor Theory

give in a reduced form below:

"Let us say we have reached the point of suddenness and are trying to predict the subsequent events. At this moment the brain is aware of the introduction and the catch, but not the solution. Each variant of the solution corresponds to an elementary outcome: y_1, y_2,...y_m. All of these outcomes together comprise a large number of possible outcomes M. When we make predictions, listening to the speaker, our brain chooses a certain number of random outcomes y_i, for which the maximum probability is $p(y_i)$. These outcomes comprise a large number of more probable outcomes K, which is a subset of M and contains k elements ($k \leq m$).

In view of limited time and the enormous m the brain cannot complete the analysis of probabilities of all of M, and therefore the size of k is much smaller than m.

Naturally, the brain doesn't use the reliable but slow algorithm of a sequential sorter. Instead, it uses some other algorithms, not fully known to us. As a result, some of the elements M that make it into K correspond to the highest probability, and some (also having high probability) don't make it in. Their probability is equated to zero, and the sum of probabilities of already evaluated events is normalized to one:

$$p'(y_j) = 0 \text{ for } y_j \notin K$$
$$\text{and}$$
$$p'(y_j) = p(y_j) / S \text{ for } y_j \notin K$$

where $S = \sum p(y_j)$ for all j where $y_j \notin K$.

This is imprecise, but the brain must content itself with this approximate but solely accessible estimation. I should say that the brain, seemingly, makes many parallel evaluations for different variants of set M. For instance, evaluations of what the next concrete word will be or what part of speech it will be: a verb or a noun, are possible.

The effect of suddenness consists in that sometimes events

y_j *occur, which were not calculated to be in set K.*

A perfectly reasonable question might arise in the reader: how will all the material provided in this Chapter lead us to the nature of humor? It doesn't seem like we were able to arrive at an understanding of the affect caused by deft wit, anecdote, couplet, caricature, or humorous tale.

Follow me, reader, and I will show you that we stand on the threshold of the discovery!

Chapter Three

Humor as a Defensive Function

From what was said in section 2.2.2. (The Aggressive Nature of Humor) we can draw the conclusion that humor is the lot of the strong and aggressive individuals of our race. But hierarchy in our society is not something that is set in stone. The battle for the top is constantly ongoing.

Those who temporarily fall to the bottom, and do not have the opportunity to joke as easily as those who stand above, are forced to use the type humor which we will call "defensive".

We will limit ourselves to four types of "defensive" humor, in which this function is clearly seen. These types are: military humor, political humor (in countries where freedom of speech is limited), Jewish humor, and that which is known as feast in the time of plague.

An appropriate analogy might be the Japanese martial art Judo, which literally translates to *"the gentle way"*. The Judoist dodges straight punches; through agility he puts his opponent into an unfavorable position from which it is easier to perform a skillful throw and gain victory over a physically superior opponent.

The types of humor examined in this chapter use the same tactic. For victory in the verbal battle one does not need to have decisive logical arguments or knowledge. The goal of comical opposition is to put the opponent into a psychologically unfavorable position while staying within the frame of safe (permissible) interaction.

Military and political humor arose from the necessity of the majority's subjection to the minority, that is, to the commanding regiment or to the government.

Jewish humor developed in a national community in one way or another isolated, barred from the ethnic and religious majority by cultural, religious and legal barriers.

A feast in time of plague, clearly, carries in itself the same defensive function of heightening the vital strength of the organism, resistance to extreme conditions.

Humor which fulfills a defensive function is not limited to these examples. We could name such types as gallows humor, corporate humor, hysterical laughter, etc.

3.1. Humor in uniform

Let's begin with a paradox: it's impossible to imagine the army without humor, just as it's impossible to imagine it without strict discipline.

Much of military humor consists of ridiculing and showing in unfavorable light those who military officers must unquestioningly obey. This is not a simple task, but often the ranking officers themselves come to aid. Young officers come to the service armed with present-day knowledge, and frequently fall under the subordination of ancient commanders. This happens especially frequently during boot camp, in which tomorrow's officers go through under the command of eternal sergeants.

Military jokes are impromptu, but many end up having a long lifespan.

Humor Theory

One commanding officer of the Kiev military school, with which the author's childhood is connected, in an attempt to give a rank of cadets with identical suitcases the uniformity recommended by regulations, once commanded: "if it is standing between the legs, put it to your side."

The major has long since departed for another world, but this phrase lives.

Another incident which occurred in the same school cost one of its participants a disciplinary penalty, despite the impeccable logic demonstrated by him.

A young officer was stopped by the school's commandant, who asked strictly:

- *Why aren't your boots shiny?*
- *Why would they be shiny, Lieutenant-Colonel?*
- *What do you mean, why? replied the taken-aback officer.*
- *Well, I haven't shined them in over a month, so why would they be shiny?*

A rather popular hero of military humor, *Gallant Soldier Joseph Švejk*, might be regarded not as an absolute negation of the particular situation - the army (the sociological aspect), and not as a "merciless criticism of the Austro-Hungarian monarchy" (the political aspect), but as the usual internal opposition of a simpler person to the "heroic" standards of behavior ascribed to him. The biggest effect is produced by the discordance of a small, comical man and a strict organization.

The heroes of military humor walk the thin line of interactions permitted by regulations. Thus, great resourcefulness needed to gain advantage under unequal conditions.

- *Whose cigar-butt is lying on the ground over there?!*
- *No one's, sir! Smoke it at your leisure!*

While hunting:

- *Hey sergeant, did I kill the rabbit?*
- *No sir! You granted it a pardon.*

3.2. Political humor

It's quite obvious that political humor is a reaction (some-times inadequate) to an overly strong concentration of power in society. It serves as an example of relatively safe liberation of pent-up aggression in regard to the authorities. Power creates institutions which aim to place various prohibitions and limita-tions on society. People seek any forms of resisting the authori-tarian impulses, and, obviously, humor is one of the most effective forms of such resistance.

Two Russians are sitting in a café. One of them is reading a magazine, on the cover of which are depicted a Rolls-Royce and an old model of a Muscovite. The other asks:
- *Which car do you like better?*
- *The Muscovite, obviously.*
- *So you know nothing about cars!*
- *No, cars I know a lot about. It's about you that I know nothing.*

Against the background of universal torpor, which seized Russian society during the period of coup of the Committee of the State of Emergency GKCP suddenly appeared a felling quip, calling to resistance:
"I had my cannon toaded light."
The author clearly remembers hearing these words a few days before the then-minister of internal affairs shot himself.

3.3. Jewish humor

In Victor Raskin's book (*Semantic Mechanisms of Humor. – Dordrecht: Reidel, 1985)* an entire section (9, chapter 6) is dedicated to this form of humor, while the entire book contains a large amount of purely Jewish jokes and anecdotes.

But first let us provide two examples, gotten from his book.

1. *The Russian ruler is inspecting the troops. He approaches a short soldier on the left flank, and demands to know his name.*
- *Muhameddinnov, Your Majesty!!!*
- *Alright, Muhameddinnov, tell me, would you be able to kill the Tsar?*
- *Hoooraaay!!! shouts the poor Turk, having poor command of the Russian language.*
   The irritated tsar approaches the tallest soldier on the right flank.
- *Name?*
- *Ivanov, Your Majesty!!!*
- *Tell me, Ivanov, would you be able to kill your Tsar?*
- *Never, Your Majesty. I'd sooner deprive myself of life; kill my parents, than ever endanger my beloved ruler, for whom each of us would be willing to lay down his life!!!*
- *Good man, Ivanov, - says the tsar, and moves on to the next group.*
- *Name?*
- *Rabinovich.*
- *Tell me, Rabinovich, would you be able to kill the tsar?*
- *What, with a drum?*
   (Russia, 1900')

2. *I told my son to marry a shiksa. If he marries a nice Jewish girl and she gets pregnant, he's going to worry like hell about her health. If she becomes fat or gets*

sick, he will be upset.

- *But a shiksa also might get pregnant, or gain weight, or...*
- *Sure, but who'd care?*
(USSR, 1930)

As we can see, defensive humor under certain conditions may lose its main function and bare "fangs and talons". Raskin, despite all this, considers Jewish humor self-deprecating. "*Jewish humor includes all ethnic jokes which have the Jews for the targeted ethnic group*". According to Raskin, "*the especially mentioned ethnic characteristics ridiculed in Jewish jokes are: sarcasm, wiliness, intelligence, cowardice, untidiness, Jewish logic, attraction to money, paradoxical relation to things, family relations (Jewish mothers and wives, and also JAP – Jewish American Princesses – that is, Jewish daughters). Also mentioned are anti-Semitism, relations with non-Jews (the goyim) and even the pogrom.*

Avner Ziv (1988) determined the purpose of Jewish humor as an aggressive-defensive mechanism. This view may be disseminated to all forms of defensive humor. A good illustration of how a defenseless person might receive an advantage from an unfavorable position could be seen in this episode of the "*Gallant Soldier Joseph Švejk*".

"*They awoke a Jew in the tavern, who began to tear his hair in regret that he cannot serve the gentlemen soldiers, and eventually began to beg them to buy his ancient, hundred year old cow, an emaciated thing, all skin and bones. He asked a fantastic sum of money for it and swore that a cow like that could not be found in all of Galicia, in all of Austria and Germany, in all of Europe, and in all the world. He howled, cried, and swore that this was the fattest cow that by Jehovah's will ever set foot on the earth. He swore by his ancestors that people came all the way from Volochinsk to see this cow; that rumors ran through the entire realm that this was not a cow, but a fairy tale, that this wasn't even a cow, but the fattest buffalo. Finally he fell before them and hugging their knees, one after another, wailed: "Kill this old unfortunate Jew, but don't leave without the cow". His wailing brought the clerk and the cook into complete confusion, and eventually they hauled off the dying beast, which no butcher would have taken a second glance at, to the field kitchen. And long after the money was in his pocket, the Jew wept that he was ruined, destroyed, robbed, having sold such a splendid cow so cheaply. He begged them to hang him for making such a mistake in his old age, for which his forefathers will be turning over in their graves. After rolling round for a little bit more in the dust, he suddenly got up, shook off all his grief, went back to his shack and told his wife: "Elsa, my life, the soldiers are idiots, and your Nathan is wise!"*

As we can see, all forms of defensive humor, including the self-deprecating, carry powerful aggressive ammunition, and serve as a weapon in the battle with a superior opponent.

3.4. Feast in time of plague

"The earthquake in Armenia greatly shook up all the soviet people".
"Time" TV program, 20 Dec. 1988

We know that it is characteristic for man to make jokes in critical and dangerous situations. Classic examples are the jokes with which famous Field Marshal **Alexander Suvorov** encouraged his soldiers. We might argue about their propriety on the battlefield, except that the great general had never in his life lost a single battle.

Academician **Dmitry Lihachev** even suggested that *"encouragement through laughter at the most pathetic moment of a deadly threat was always a purely Russian national phenomenon."*

It is well known fact that the soldiers who spent a long time in entrenchments, in dampness, and in freezing weather seldom fell victim to catarrhal diseases. They sneezed, coughed, but almost no one landed in a hospital with influenza or an acute respiratory condition. Clearly, in extreme conditions, the sub-conscious defense mechanisms turn on, including humor. In dangerous situations this defense mechanism turns on auto-matically, subconsciously.

The author had to survive an event, the scale of which might be compared to the Black Plague. The event in question is the accident at the atomic station near Chernobyl.

When on the morning of April 26, 1986 we heard about the "explosion" at the Chernobyl reactor, the first reaction was, as it is imprinted in memory, a laughter. Horror, fear of the uncer-tainty came later, but in the beginning, there was laughter. And it didn't stop for many months in the entire city of Kiev (50 miles from Chernobyl), which was covered by a radioactive cloud on the eve of First of May Day. This was an unforgetta-ble time. Conversations, discussions, arguments on the bus, in a subway, at work, in companies, in bed all revolved around the same subject. Everything else stopped existing. The situa-tion was made more difficult by the fact that the government found nothing better to do than to kill all sources of informa-tion and even ban the sale of instruments to measure levels of radioactivity, previously held in the Civil Defense divisions of any significantly large enterprise.

In response, multiple anecdotes, jokes, and ditties ap-peared, most of them dedicated to one of two themes: the ex-pected reduction of potency in men, and the undoubted role of alcohol in suppressing the effects of radiation.

Two weeks after the explosion, on May 8th 1986 the author was coming off the plane in the Litovian airport, the first phrase he heard from the crowd of those meeting him was the ditty:

Humor Theory

A "Zaporojetz" is no car
A Kievian is no man.

Zaporozhets ne mashina,
Kievlyanin – ne muzshina.

The men of Kiev did not remain in debt, and tried with all their might to prove the falsity of this accusation. The sexual aggression in the city drastically increased. But the amount of laughter increased even more. In the Institute hallways, one could hear peals, even explosions of laughter constantly emanating from behind the closed doors of laboratories and offices.

The city laughed!!! And we survived.

Chapter Four

Classification of Humor

The first attempts to classify wit go back to hoar antiquity: they were undertaken by **Cicero** and **Quintillian**.

Cicero relied on his experience as a public speaker. In his treatise "*The Orator*" he grouped all forms of wit into two different types:

1. Funniness that comes of the nature of the object itself.
2. The verbal form of wit, which includes:
   - absurdity
   - ambiguity
   - unexpected conclusions
   - puns
   - allegory
   - contrast
   - apparent simplicity
   - caricature

- comparison (similarity)
- contradiction (contrast)
- unresolved expectation
- evasiveness
- irony
- metaphor
- mockery
- tall tales
- sayings
- light mockery
- unexpectedness
- underestimation
- literal understanding of words
- unusual interpretation of proper nouns

This is the first formal classification of wit. You can imagine with what mastery and, apparently, practical results the great orator used these methods.

Quintillian also examined wit in relation to rhetoric. He separated witticisms from mere funny statements more clearly than did Cicero. He understood that people laugh not only at witticisms, but also at stupidity, cowardice, lack of restraint, and so forth.

Quintillian divided all of the reasons which cause smiling and laughter into six groups:

1. Refinement (urbalitas).
2. Grace (venustum).
3. Piquancy (salsum).
4. Joke (facetum)
5. Witticism (jocus)
6. Good-natured teasing (decacitas).

Alexander Luk classified the methods of wit known to him as follows:

1. False contrast
2. False strengthening
3. Driving to absurdity:
   a. Exaggeration (hyperbole)
   b. Understatement or softening (euphemism)
4. Witticism of absurdity:
   a. The connection of two logically incompatible statements
   b. Paralogistic conclusion
5. Mixing of styles or "combination of plans":
   a. Mixing of vocal styles
   b. Metaphorical terminology
   c. Incompatibility of style and content
   d. Incompatibility of the style of speech and the situation in which it's uttered
   e. Pseudo-profundity
6. A hint, or a precise chain of associations
7. Double meaning
   a. Play on words
   b. Ambiguity
8. Irony
9. Backward comparison
   a. "Pure" backward comparison
   b. Literalization of a metaphor
10. Comparison through a random or secondary characteristic, the enumeration of incompatible subjects in the same list.
11. Repetition
    a. "Pure" repetition
    b. Repetition with a change in grammatical construction
    c. Repetition with a change in meaning.
12. Paradox

Victor Raskin differentiates the verbal forms of the funny in the following manner (incomplete list):

1. Ridicule
    Who was that gentleman that I saw you with last evening?
    He's not a gentleman, he's a senator!
2. Self-mockery

A man condemned to the firing squad on Monday: "What a way to start the week".

3. Self-disparaging humor
4. Riddle
5. Word play

- *What is the first thing a person runs into when he gets to New York for the first time?*
- *An automobile.*

Thomas C. Veatch in his "*A Theory of Humor*" gives the following (also incomplete) list of the types of the funny:

1. Driving to absurdity
2. Satire
3. Literal interpretation of a metaphor
4. Irony
5. Double meaning
6. Contradiction
7. Incompatibility
8. Withdrawal from danger
9. Establishment of superiority
10. Excessive rationality
11. Excessive rationality
12. Deviation from the commonplace
13. Others

Miroslav Voinarovsky (http://psi-logic.narod.ru/steb/steb.htm, in Russian) divides the funny into the following categories:

1. *Anix* (term introduced by Voinarovsky)
2. Pun
3. The grotesque
4. Double meaning
5. Reversing
6. Association
7. Transferring
8. Omission
9. Repetition
10. Reduction
11. Interpretation
12. Hint
13. Incompleteness
14. Euphemism
15. Rhyme (with a hint at impropriety).

A common thread in these interpretations is that they don't track internal, fundamental differences clearly enough. They don't pretend to scientific nature. A scientific classification of the forms of humor must be based not on a list of the forms, but on the grouping of the methods or forms by general essential characteristics. The deeper we can penetrate the essence of the funny, the more logical, and, as a rule, the simpler the classification will be. Ideally, the scientific classification will consist of only two divisions.

One such classification exists and belongs to Sigmund Freud, who differentiated jokes and the comic in the following way: *"A joke is invented; the comic happens"*.

Raskin similarly differentiated *intentional* and *unintentional* humor, which is close to the conclusion of Freud.

The author of the present investigation thinks that there are more than enough arguments in favor of the aggressive nature of humor, the point of view that <u>humor is always used as an intellectual weapon in the fight for increasing one's social status, or as preparation for intellectual combat; training of a sort, a warm-up.</u> Social status is not measured in absolute units. It is the position of a person relative to other individuals. An increase of social status can come about in only two ways: an increase of one's own status, or the decreasing of the social status of those surrounding. On the basis of this view, a universal classification of the funny might go as follows:

1. Humor of deprecation. We are gladdened; we think it's funny when someone gets into a compromising position.
2. Humor of elevation. We receive pleasure when we are elevated in our own eyes or in the eyes of others.
3. Mixed humor. This is a combination of the previous two.

It's not hard to see that all three types of the funny can be used for advancement up the social ladder, fixation of reached positions, or for training our abilities to combat others. This mental training seems harmless, and has led many scholars to the conclusion about the existence of inoffensive jokes, not causing anyone harm. Similarly, fencing lessons, archery, and boxer training might all seem inoffensive; everything depends on the point of view and realization of the knowledge received at these lessons.

It is interesting that the aggressive nature of three out of the four known types of the funny: *satire, sarcasm, irony and humor*, is not doubted. And it's only apropos humor do opinions diverge. Many believe that there exists a harmless form of humor, not targeted at anyone's deprecation or elevation. We will try and show that there exists a different viewpoint on this form of the funny.

Let us provide a few examples.

4.1. Humor of deprecation

A pure example of the humor of deprecation is mockery of

a person who got into an awkward position or who possesses physical deficiencies. For example, *"Oh, look at that hair! Has it gone all rusty? Did your parents leave you out in the rain?"* Such humor was used by clowns on the arena. The white-haired clown smacks the red-haired clown on the head, he trips, spills a bucket of water on himself, gets into a pickle. Situational comedy, especially silent movies, over which we laughed ourselves to tears, almost entirely consists of such humor. Here's an example:

D. Minaev

A mongrel loped down Nevsky Avenue
Behind, Burenin quietly ran
Oh, guard the dog, monsignor policeman
From the menace of the biting man!

Po Nevskomu bezhit sobaka,
Za ney Burenin, tih I mil...
Gorodovoy, smotri, odnako,
Chtob on eyo ne ukusil!

In this epigram, there is almost nothing of the riddles inherent to humor, no "shining contradiction", except perhaps for a small exaggeration that a case of man biting dog is improbable. This is a typical example of depreciating humor. Notice, however, that without this small contradiction, this epigram would have been flat and simply fall out of the category of humor.

4.2. Humor of elevation

Alexander Ivanov to Maya Plisetskaya (famous Bolshoi Theater ballerina)

Humor Theory

Of you, I'll always speak enthralled,
Impromptu, and with charm;
Your legs to keep, the Bolshoi's halls
Would give up their right arms.

Ya govorit' o vas bi mog
Ekspromtom I ne vdrug;
Bol'shoy teatr bez vashih nog
Bukval'no kak bez ruk.

It would seem that aggression is nowhere to be found in this epigram. It is certainly flattering to the woman addressed. But aggression is indeed present here. The brilliantly written epigram elevates simultaneously the author, the reader, and the great ballerina. The image of Maya Plisetskaya is elevated through refined flattery. The author secures his position as leader of national parody and epigram. The reader's status rises as well, though to a lesser degree. All this becomes evident with a simple alteration of the text. Let us remove the element of humor from this epigram. For instance:

Of you, I'll always speak enthralled,
Impromptu, and with charm;
For you, the Bolshoi's vaulted halls
Would give up their right arms.

Ya govorit' mogu seychas
Ekspromtom I ne vdrug:
Boyus', Bol'shoy teatr bez vas
Bukval'no, kak bez ruk.

The meaning of the epigram is the same; the same amount of flatter and admiration is present. But the play on words *"legs-arms"* has disappeared – and the reader literally feels duped. He has nothing to think about; nothing to puzzle out. The element of mental gymnastics is no longer present. The author is automatically cast into the set of tedious rhymes. And the readers don't get the same impulse of elevation or self-delight that they do from the classic epigram of Alexander Ivanov. The cited epigram is a classis case of the humor of elevation. It allows the reader to feel himself "on the level", and sometimes even above the level if we happen to hear this epigram in the presence of someone who didn't get it.

Another example of pure elevating wit is the following couplet by **Alexander Pope**:

> *Nature and nature's laws lay hid in night;*
> *God said 'Let Newton be' and all was light.*

to which **Sir John Collings Squire** later added:

> *It did not last: the devil, shouting 'Ho.*
> *Let Einstein be' restored the status quo.*

4.3. Mixed humor

Lord Alfred Tennyson began a *"To E. L. on his Travels in Greece"* as follows:

> *Illyrian woodlands, echoing falls*
> *Of water, sheets of summer glass,*
> *The long divine Peneian pass,*
> *The vast Akrokeraunian walls,*

> *Tomohrit, Athos, all things fair,*
> *With such a pencil, such a pen,*
> *You shadow forth to distant men,*
> *I read and felt that I was there:*

Humor Theory

The recipient of the tribute, the great parodist **Edward Lear** wrote his own version of the poem:

> *Delirious Bulldogs; -- echoing calls*
> *My daughter, -- green as summer grass; --*
> *The long supine Plebeian ass,*
> *The nasty crockery boring falls; --*
>
> *Tom-Moory Pathos; -- all things bare, --*
> *With such a turkey! such a hen!*
> *And scrambling forms of distant men,*
> *O! ain't you glad you were not there!*

In this parody, not only is the author of the poem lightly mocking the original poem, but also himself (as the beneficiary of the original). At the same time, the status of the author is elevated through his clever manipulation of words and meaning. The reader's status is similarly elevated through solving the simple mapping between the parody and the original. This is humor of the mixed type; a multi-dimensional parody comprised of both deprecation (of the parodied author) and elevation (of the author and the reader).

Chapter Five

Humor Theory

*The human race has one really
effective weapon, and that is laughter*
Mark Twain

I n the previous chapters we accumulated enough evidence
to allow us to make clear the state of present-day investigations in the field of the funny. We have everything we need
in order to embark on an orderly and systematic search for the
answer to the main question: **"Why does a person laugh?"**
We won't concern ourselves with the question **"when?"** or
"under what conditions", but merely **"why?"** And also:
"what for?"

For we have not encountered answers to these basic questions.

Humor Theory

In **chapter 2** we came to the following conclusions:

- Humor exists as an objective phenomenon.
- Humor has an aggressive nature. A person laughs not only at "innocent" jokes, but also at the misfortunes of others.
- The percentage of natural jokers and natural leaders is approximately the same.
- A sense of humor is something vitally important to a human being.
- Humor can be divided into two basic types: the *humor of elevation*, and the *humor of deprecation*. If these two types are both present, we get *mixed humor*.

To find the answer, we need the following statements, which we call - **13 Theses**. The reader won't find anything new in them. These theses are, as a matter of fact, borrowed from existing works and have undergone only the slightest rephrasing. An overwhelming majority of the scholars would agree with them:

1. Humor is an innate phenomenon, and plays an essential role in the survival of the species.
2. Humor is not the most complex, but one of the most primitive of emotions. There are evidences that humor is innate in primates and other animals.
3. Smiles, laughter, exploding with mirth, brought by a wit, are all expressions of pleasure.
4. Any joke is characterized by certain illogicality, a "shining contradiction", a riddle, separating it from the usual logical thought.
5. Pleasure from humor is reached from gaining either
    a. superiority over another, or

        b.   intellectual triumph from solving the riddle, thus…

6. "A keen word said twice becomes dull." (**Alexander Pushkin**)
7. An audience reacts more enthusiastically to jokes if it is in a good mood.
8. An orator laughs at a joke he knows well with greater pleasure than the audience.
9. Humor is perceived differently (frequently with opposite signs) by the joker and the audience, and the person or persons being ridiculed; by the "aggressor" and his listeners on one side, and the "object of aggression" on the other.
10. A well-done joke can elevate or offend a person to whom it's addressed more so than a flat joke.
11. Humor is a social phenomenon, an intellectual weapon. It doesn't exist outside of the human factor. Humor is a weapon of aggression in the strong, and fulfills a defensive function in the weak.
12. The greatest effect is reached if the time spent solving the "riddle" is small.
13. For the best apprehension of the joke, the listener should be prepared (forewarned).

Humor is a primitive phenomenon (**theses 1** and **2**). It is accessible to everyone, even to children and savages. Its nature has, most likely, a similarly simple, primitive explanation. It is this very sort of explanation that we are to arrive at, not even arrive at: not overlook. As it will be shown below, this solution has already been located by our predecessors. They had one additional small step to make; the last stride to the finish line.

Laughter is an expression of pleasure (**thesis 3**). A pure instance of the <u>laughter of deprecation</u> is free from riddles, from the "shining contradiction". This primitive, rough humor presents no mystery to us. This laughter manifests from the satisfaction of purely aggressive, low feelings, self-elevation at the price of the humiliation of others. We could pretend that we are not subject to such humor, that misfortunes that happen to our enemies leave us with discomfort and entirely unpleasant feelings. Of course, in that case we would have to ignore a couple of things. Ignore the thunderous laughter of the audience while watching slapstick silent films; forget our childish glee at the site of clowns on the circus arena, who got into funny situations with falling and spilling water on themselves. We'll forget these things as a distant dream, and move on to the more refined forms of the funny. According to our classification system, there are only two: the humor of elevation, and mixed humor.

Every joke of the <u>humor of elevation</u> contains an intellectual "riddle" (**thesis 4**) which we must solve. Laughter testifies of the pleasure we gain from successfully accomplishing the mental task – the solving of the "riddle" (**thesis 5 b**). For instance, the simple reversal of words or their incorrect usage frequently becomes funny, as we are offered the mental challenge: restore the logical order of the words and understand their intended meaning. If there is no riddle, or the answer to it is known ahead of time, we have nothing to solve. The joke stops being funny (**thesis 6**). Regular jokers frequently use this method. They simply switch around the words in a phrase or place unexpected synonyms in well-known idioms. If a person replaces just one word in a heavily used phrase: "*Make a mountain out of a molehill*" and instead says "*make a mountain out of a brass farthing*" he might pass as a comedian.

Thesis 4 is considered to be correct by a majority of investigators. **Quintillian** wrote "*And by Hercules, the entire purpose of a joke is to express reality in a different way: this is done by warping one's own or someone else's convictions or by saying something impossible*".

And this is how **Arthur Schopenhauer** expressed the same idea in his book "*The World as Will and Representation*", (1819): "*Laughter always signifies the sudden appre-*

hension of an incongruity between a concept and the real object thought through it, and represents a mere expression of this incongruity." The key word here is *"unexpected"* or *"sudden".* It will be explained below why.

Let us label the value which designates the level of Pleasure received from Solving the Riddle with the abbreviation **PSR**. This pleasure may be strong, weak, or entirely nonexistent. The value of **PSR** may be expressed as several variables. We will formalize these variables below.

The listeners' mood elevates the effect of humor (**thesis 7**). When in a good mood, people laugh more willingly; it's easier to make them laugh. The level of the mood can also be expressed as a variable. We shall call this value the Background Mood (**BM**). The Pleasure received from Solving the Riddle is superimposed on the Background Mood. The Effect of Humor is the sum of these two values. This gives us the basis for constructing the initial expression for the Effect of Humor (**EH**).

$$EH = PSR + BM, \qquad (1)$$

where **EH** = the effect of humor,
   PSR = the pleasure gained from solving the riddle, and
   BM = the background mood.

For the formula to make sense, we must assign some (even conditional) values for evaluating its components and designate their value ranges. Fortunately for us, an anonymous Russian folk had already done this work before us, having established the unit of **EH**. This unit he labeled as **"laughter"**, and gave it a quantitative value of one arbitrary unit. This unit is mentioned in **V. I. Dal**'s Russian Language Dictionary: *"Laughter for all, but not even a half-laugh for us".*

Let us also designate the maximum possible pleasure received from the apprehension of a joke as **1 Laugh**, or **1 L** for short. A value of 1.0 L will correspond to the largest possible value of **EH**, which in plain speak is called a horse-laugh or "rolling on the floor laughing". It's not hard to see that the values of **PSR** and **BM** must have the same units (L). Let us set an arbitrary maximum for **PSR** equal to the maximum value of **BM**, that is, at 0.5 L. Such a value of **BM** corresponds to a very joyous state of the soul, such that it's very easy to make the person laugh. To do this it is enough to use the ancient folk method of adding a slight value of +1.0 F (one finger) to the level of **BM**. As a limitation, let us assume that this finger is not the middle one. When this happens, the value of **EH** will exceed the ground state; that is, the conditions for laughter will have been created.

The maximum value of **PSR**, equal to +0.5 L, corresponds to the first-rate joke, such as a fresh, timely, and well-told anecdote.

The minimal value of **PSR** = -0.5 L (a blasphemous, offensive joke). The minimum value of BM = -0.5L, which corresponds to such deep depression that even a dose of +2.0 F won't raise the mood to a sufficient laughter. In such depression, even the most successful joke with a value of PSR = +0.5L won't cause more than a slight sad movement of the lips. The total value of **EH** will be close to zero (0.0 L).

The maximal possible value of **EH** equals 1.0 L, and the minimal is -1.0 L. Despite the arbitrariness of the values adopted by us, this approach will allow us to avoid vague judgments and will enable us to compare conclusions.

Formula (1) introduces nothing new into our understanding of the nature of the funny; it is simply a conditional mathematical illustration of known positions. Despite its inevitable subjectivity, it gives us the opportunity for numerical analysis. However, this formula did not put us any closer to the answer to the following important questions:

1. Why does the orator, for whom the pleasure gained from solving the riddle (**thesis 6**) presents no effort (PSR = 0), receives a greater pleasure from his joke than the audience (**thesis 8**)? At the

same time, the listener who is well acquainted with the joke and has already solved this riddle receives no pleasure (EH = 0).

2. For the object of aggression or mockery, solving the riddle comprising the salt of the joke brings no pleasure at all (EH < 0, **thesis 9**). On the contrary, a well-aimed joke is capable of causing a stronger negative or positive reaction than a weak joke (**thesis 10**). How can we explain why a successful jibe that hit the target causes a stronger negative reaction from the ridiculed than an unsuccessful, flat mockery?

3. Why do we obtain pleasure from solving the elementary, simple riddles and contradictions that comprise the salt of the jokes? Why does this simple intellectual exercise bring about an influx of happiness, accompanied by laughter, and the solution of other more complex and prestigious problems rarely call laughter forth?

The answers to these three questions will lead us to the solution of the eternal riddle: **"Why we laugh"**.

We notice that the information included in the three questions highlighted by us is not the fruit of our conclusions or imagination. Anyone can recognize its validity from his experience. But a convincing, logical answer to these questions has not yet been given.

Answer to the First question

We have arrived at the conclusion that humor has as its goal obtaining or maintaining a certain advantage in society (**theses 5 a** and **11**). Most researchers are in agreement on this point.

Thomas Hobbes (1588-1679) maintained that laughter is caused by a feeling of superiority over some subject. He used the term *"sudden triumph"*. We turn the reader's attention to the word *"triumph"*, and note its accompanying word *"sudden"*. Four centuries ago, Thomas Hobbes had been very close to the solution of humor.

His predecessor **Giangorno Trissino** (1478-1550) wrote in his theses *"Poetica"*: *"this* (humor) *brings pleasure thanks to the fact that man is by nature envious and malevolent"*.

If Thomas Hobbes and his numerous followers were right, then we must part with one strongly rooted illusion: namely that humor serves merely to bring pleasure and entertainment. In fact, **the value of EH, the effect of humor, is expressed by none other than the success in one's advancement up the social ladder.** This success may be evinced through receiving a certain status in society, signs of approval and admiration, attentions of the opposite sex and other things which are so valued by people in this life. The purpose of humor as a phenomenon consists precisely of this and none other.

The Effect of Humor = A Change in Social Status.

This is the answer to the <u>first</u> of the questions we are facing. Humor serves not only to cheer up an audience or to spend time merrily. The value of **EH** will be maximal not when a joke is elegantly and skillfully composed, not when anecdote is masterfully told, but only in <u>that case</u> when the narrator and the listener receive as a result some sort of an advantage over others; advance up the social ladder of the group, collective, or family, or if they maintain their position.

A regular joker, a skillful teller of anecdotes, a person whose speech is sprinkled with skillful turns, a speaker who gives color to the content of his speech with jokes all have a greater chance of attracting attention to themselves and gaining success than a person who presents his thoughts flatly, "without a raisin". It is the orator who gets the applause.

The listeners increase their status by demonstrating their ability to solve intellectual problems (**thesis 5 b**) and erudition, the ability to easily orient themselves in the sea of information necessary for solving the problem. Therefore, as experimental studies testify and everyday experience backs up, the teller receives greater enjoyment and laughs more merrily and infectiously than the listeners.

We are participants in an ongoing competition with others like ourselves for a place under the sun. A successful witticism or a positive reaction to a joke is equivalent to scoring a point in a tennis match or a well-cued billiard ball. These humble sportive achievements are the straight analogies of a successful joke. Each point and each ball scored elevates us in our own eyes, and in the eyes of those surrounding.

Each joke does the same with us.
And nothing more!

The process of apprehending a joke or anecdote could be imagined in the following way. The narrator throws certain objects to the audience: balls, or Frisbees, which listeners try to catch. Some participants catch the objects quickly and with skill, some clumsily, and some miss the objects entirely or drop them on the floor. Is this light, easy entertainment? Sure, but it's a competitive entertainment. The participants try to not land with their face in the mud, and to show off their skill to others.

Even a friendly match on the tennis court almost always turns into a scored game, and not just a simple tossing of the ball back and forth. A gained point always generates pleasure, while a skillfully returned ball – not always. For this reason the number of tennis lovers who play with their partners is much greater than the number of people who like bouncing the balls against a wall.

Let us look at the following example:

Humor Theory

Yuriy Tynyanov

Pushkin willed us "Liberty"
And Gogol thumbed his "Nose"
Turgenev wrote back, "Uberty!"
"Good-s", Mayakovsky goes.

Ostavil Pushkin odu "Vol'nost'",
A Gogol' natyanul nam "Nos".
Turgenev napisal "Dovol'no",
A Mayakovskiy – "Horosho-s".

Let's imagine that this epigram was read in English speaking company, where not everyone has read Mayakovsky or studied for exams based on his poem *"Good!"* Will they understand the meaning of the last line of the epigram? We can probably assume that the classic epigram won't seem funny to this audience. On the other hand, those who are well familiar with Mayakovsky's and Tynyanov's writing and their complex biographies will get a great deal to think about from these four lines: comparisons, the propriety of the suffix –"s". These listeners will get a positive psychological impulse, elevating them in their own eyes and over those in the audience who did not understand the epigram.

For those readers already familiar with Tynyanov's epigram, this won't call forth a smile. But even they would have felt pleasure from hearing it in diverse company because they would have felt themselves on top, having remembered all of its nuances, and having exchanged auguring smiles with the other such knowledgeable listeners, would have added themselves to the highest part of those present. But the greatest success falls to the part of the author of the epigram. Can he hold back his pleasure of success, even if this epigram has been told multiple times?

The purpose of the humoristic process as we've defined it (the elevation of social status) gives us an answer to the **first** of

88

the questions set before us.

Answer to the Second question

In accordance to what has been said, and relying on **thesis 9**, it would be logical to modify Formula (1). According to the ideas of **Henri Bergson** and other researchers, (*"the funny is connected either to something human or to something related or able to be ascribed to humanity"*) humor does not exist separately from the human factor. Indeed, let us imagine the following situations. The first: **Charlie Chaplin** swings the ladder that he's carrying on his shoulder at a negative character, and the latter falls into a bucket of gunk. This is funny. Situation the second: the same swing lands on the head of a blind girl from the movie *"City Lights"*. Is this funny? No, it's more likely that the audience won't like this and get angry. Finally, the third situation: Chaplin strikes a brick wall with that same ladder. How does the audience respond? They don't, really; they don't care. Three of the same actions, and three entirely different reactions from the audience.

To obtain the effect of the funny, the listener must be personally involved in the experience. A person who is obviously deformed or a lame soccer player chasing a ball calls forth laughter. But a crooked brick, or a brick with a chipped off corner isn't funny. Nothing that happens to the brick can cause the comic effect. The comic effect can only be reached if the brick falls on someone's head, or if the anecdote begins with the words: *"Two bricks are crawling along..."* In these cases we get a connection with humans, or analogy with human behavior.

But the bricks that lie there without motion and don't crawl anywhere cannot cause a comic effect. Why? Simply because we can't morally rise above the bricks. But if we're told that a brick lies on top of another, this might call forth a well-known analogy, and could become the start of an anecdote or caricature.

To reach the effect of the funny, it is necessary for the listener to feel empathy towards the subjects of the joke.

The listener feels emotions due to Personal Empathy (**PE**) to these subjects. The listener can feel superior over the heroes of the joke or anecdote. This elevates him in his own eyes. On the other hand, the listener (as in the example of Maya Plisetskaya) may feel empathy towards a favorite ballerina, and become elevated along with her. In both cases, empathy increases the effect of the joke. The value of **PE** in this case will be positive. If the joke offends the listener, rubs him the wrong way or insults his close ones (like the honor of his wife), the value of **PE** will be negative. In those cases where the listener feels no empathy towards the subject of the joke, the value of **PE** will be equal to zero, and the joke won't seem funny. For example, in the nineties, a popular joke in America was the following, heard on the Johnny Carson radio show: *"Why did the vice-president go to Panama?" "Because the shooting there had stopped."* We understand the salt of the joke. It's not hard to guess that the cowardice of the vice president is being ridiculed. But someone who wasn't living in America at that time might have trouble remembering who the vice-president was; the personal qualities of that vice-president affect the person about as much as the behavior of a stationary brick. As a result, the joke isn't funny for this person. But Americans of the time loved it.

It would be logical therefore to add in the term reflecting Personal Empathy into Formula (1):

$$EH = PE + PSR + BM, \qquad (2)$$

However, according to **thesis 10**, the value of **PE** depends on the success of the joke. A keen joke can rub us the wrong or right way, whereas a flat joke can neither cheer us up nor offend us. It would be quite logical therefore to express the first two terms in Formula (2) not as a sum, but as a product. The formula of the funny then takes on the following form:

$$EH = PE * PSR + BM, \qquad\qquad (3)$$
where * is the multiplication sign, and **PE** becomes unitless.

To maintain the value boundaries set by us for **EH** (± 1.0 L), let us give **PE** a maximal value of $+1.0$, and a minimal of -1.0. Notice that the minimal value of **PSR** is now equal to zero (a flat joke) and the maximum remains 0.5 L as before. The maximum value of **EH**, 1.0L, can be reached under the following conditions:

- The joke is successful. PSR = +0.5 L.
- The narrator received the maximal possible benefits from the related (or conceived) joke: Homeric laughter, applause, shouts of "bravo", amorous smiles of beautiful women, etc. PE = +1.0. The listeners have gotten a healthy amount of malicious rejoicing over the unlucky hero of the joke (for them PE also = +1.0).
- The mood of the audience is most favorable. The narrator is well-known and beloved by the audience; the listeners expect humor of the highest class from him. They are "warmed up" by the setting or by alcoholic substances. The value of BM = +0.5 L.

In this case, EH = PE * PSR + BM = +1.0 * (+0.5L) + 0.5 L = +1.0 L.

The minimal value of **EH**, equal to -1.0 L might be reached under the following conditions:

- The joke is quite astute; it hit the mark. PSR = +0.5 L.
- With his joke, the narrator has managed to awaken quite unpleasant associations. For instance, maybe

he told an anecdote about a rope in the house of a man who hung himself. Perhaps religious or nationalistic beliefs were infringed upon. The value of PE = -1.0.

- The mood of the audience was very low. Something very unpleasant had just happened (BM = -0.5 L).

The value of EH = PE + PSR + BM = -1.0 * (+0.5 L) – 0.5 L = -1.0 L

The result of a negative **EH** might be silent disapproval, or in extreme cases, expulsion from the room, with a strict order never to return. Cries of "boo!", "shame on you!", "out!", "never come back, you asshole!" accompany the expulsion.

Note that in the case of a flat joke (PSR = 0), the minimal value of **EH** is only
- 0.5 L:

EH = PE * PSR + BM = -1.0 * (0.0 L) – 0.5 L = -0.5 L.

An **EH** value of zero (0.0 L) might be achieved as a result of a combination of different circumstances. For example, the joke might be quite successful; the narrator received the acknowledgement of the audience, but the general mood (BM < 0) is not favorable for laughter.

EH = PE * PSR + BM = 1.0 * (0.5 L) – 0.5 L = 0.0 L.

The readers can mentally reproduce a familiar life situation, a successful or unsuccessful attempt to joke, and get an estimation of the EH for themselves using the proposed procedure. Formula (3) shows that laughter is produced only when the object of the joke is not indifferent to us. This formula expresses the idea of A. Bergson mathematically. It gives a simplified visual approximation of the interdependence between the quality of the joke and the effect caused by it. It also gives a quantitative relationship, illustrating the answer to the **second** of the questions posed by us.

In the majority of the cases, the value **PE** has a negative value for the object of the joke. The overall **EH** of the person being ridiculed will be the lower, the better the joke, and the more hostile is the mood of the audience. A typical audience is predisposed to dislike unpleasant people, people who undeservedly achieved success such as aristocrats; and some audience simply dislikes wealthy people. Such an audience gleefully reacts to situations in which a similar character gets into an awkward situation. To express ourselves mathematically, the value **PE** for the listeners will always be greater than zero. Thus, the same joke can either have a positive or a negative effect, depending on whether the social status of the persons attending this joke is elevated or deprecated.

As an illustration, let us examine the following anecdote:

The newest computer model, able to answer any question, was demonstrated to a skeptical British lord.

The lord asked: "What is my father doing right now?"

Computer: "Right now your father is fishing on the shores of the Thames."

The lord triumphantly takes a telegram out of the pocket of his secretary: "Lord Bartell left yesterday for a resort in Nice."

The computer answers: "Lord Bartell left yesterday for a resort in Nice. And your father is catching fish on the shores of the Thames."

How successful is this anecdote? Clearly, the value **PSR** will be high for most listeners. Let us give it a value of +0.3 L. The values of **PE** and **EH**, on the other hand, will heavily depend on the audience to which the joke is told. In democratic circles, the value of **PE** will be close to 1.0 and the value of **EH** might reach almost maximal parameters: +0.8 L. But if the narrator had the stupidity to tell this joke in aristocratic circles, the anecdote might seem tactless (no kidding!) and the narrator will be expelled. The minimal value of **EH** may reach

$$EH = PE * PSR + BM = -1.0 * (+0.3 \text{ L}) - 0.5 \text{ L} = -0.8 \text{ L}$$

In this case, the aristocratic circle becomes the object of aggression, as well as the very principle of the inheritance of aristocratic titles. In the closets of all, even the most aristocratic family, is at least one skeleton, and the goal of aggression aimed at the degradation if their social status will have been reached. And the **EH** will be higher, the more successful the anecdote. It is noteworthy that the negative value of **EH** of the aristocrats will be achieved through a positive characteristic of the joke (PSR > 0).

More about defensive humor, or the skill of changing the sign

We have postulated above that for the object of ridicule, the value **PE** is always negative. Such a person is the object of aggression, and if the joke at his expense causes the laughter of others, his social status decreases (EH < 0). But there are exceptions. A person able to laugh at himself, and who does this naturally, can elevate his social status and change the sign of **PE** to the opposite. In this case, the impression is created in those surrounding that the teasing is only tribute to the popularity of the person, and he himself is far above the small digs contained in the jibe.

If the anecdote examined above is told in a family of aristocrats who have adhered to conservative traditions since the beginning of time and are absolutely convinced of the uprightness of their genealogical tree, this anecdote might have some success. In this case, the attack directed at the family will ricochet and even bring the members a good deal of pleasure if it happens to land on the neighbors. Their social status will be elevated even higher- over their aristocrat-neighbors. Then the maximal value of **EH** will be the same as it was in the democratic circles:

$$EH = PE * PSR + BM = 1.0 * (+0.3\ L) + 0.5\ L = 0.8\ L$$

This effect (changing the sign of **PE**) is a characteristic property of the "defensive humor" examined in Chapter 3. A narrator who uses such humor intentionally lowers his status to get the audience on his side, to allow it to feel superior over him. The pleasure received by the audience calls up sympathy towards the narrator, since it's pleasant for the listeners to be in the company of a person who elevates their social status. As a result, the gained sympathy can be used by the skillful orator for his own means.

Let us give an example, which we scooped up from the September issue of *Reader's Digest* (2004, pg. 105). A real estate agent, and a Manhattan multimillionaire, **Barbara Corcoran** is obliged to both her intelligence, and a well-timed joke for her success. Many years ago, when Barbara managed to get an interview with the rich and powerful **Donald Trump**, she told the latter: *"My husband is a pale imitation of you."* *Reader's Digest* doesn't mention what exactly gave her the basis for this conclusion, but the joke was successful. Mr. Trump was so delighted that he remembered this phrase and quoted it publicly after a conference with other businessmen, two years after the memorable meeting. Soon after this, Mr. Trump entrusted Ms. Corcoran with selling 8 blocks of real estate constructed by him. The commissions from the sales totaled two million dollars. Afterwards, Barbara sold her company for 66 million, while managing to remain on as president. She expressed the lesson learned as follows: *"If you laugh at others, you are pushing people away from you. But if you laugh at yourself, people have the immediate urge to come to your aid."*

From the point of view of our theory, the clever Barbara merely learned to flip the sign of **PE** to the opposite. This comes as no surprise: her childhood was passed in a poor Irish family, and all of life's lessons she absorbed in along with her mother's milk who managed to raise ten children and teach them the everyday wisdom of flipping the sign.

It's quite clear that even the simplified approach expressed in Formula (3) is convenient for illustrating basic positions, and quite successfully addresses the second of the posed questions. **Thesis 11** becomes completely clear.

Answer to the Third question

For finding the answer to the third and final question, we need nothing more than simple logical thought. For it was here that our predecessors, without exception, have stopped. We know (**thesis 4**) that each joke contains a certain intellectual riddle which the listener is offered to solve. The presence of the riddle separates the funny from the non-funny. This is a necessary condition. Laughter is caused by pleasure from having solved the riddle (**thesis 5 b**). We also know (**thesis 12**) that the time spent on solving the riddle should be small. But we don't know why. The answer to this question is simple and... almost obvious, but its understanding demands a prior explanation.

Let us remember a few examples from elementary physics.

1. Someone is stroking your hand, or is giving you a massage, or (if you're a woman) is gently squeezing your breast. In the majority of cases, such touch gives you pleasant sensations. But if someone applies equal force to a needle whose point is resting on your flesh, the sensation becomes painful and unpleasant. The same force **F** is pressing on a much smaller area **A**. Pressure **P**, that is, the quotient resulting from dividing the force by the area is equal to:

$$P = F/A \qquad (4)$$

The smaller the area **A**, the larger the pressure P, and the more unpleasant the sensation will be. The area of the needle's point is much smaller than the area of the palm, and the value of the pressure will be large even with a small applied force.

2. Everyone knows the natural phenomena known as lightning, and the destructive consequences which it can lead to. Lighting has colossal power. With a voltage which can reach up ten million volts, and a current up to twenty thousand amperes, the power **Pp** of a lightning strike exceeds 200 thousand million watts. This is equal to the power of 400 legendary Dnieper Dam in the Ukraine.

Lightning appears as a result of an accumulation of charges in the upper atmosphere. These charges rise there from the lower atmosphere. Electric current which delivers the chargers to the upper levels of the atmosphere flows without interruption. What is the value of the current directed upwards from the entire surface of the Earth, from all its 450 million square kilometers? It's surprising, but the value of the current from this entire area is only around 1000 amperes, that is, 20 times less than the amplitude of the current flowing down the narrow channel of a single lighting bolt. And Earth gets about 16 million thunderstorms each year.

Such a great difference between the unimaginable power **Pp** of the atmospheric charge and the modest value **Pa** of the accumulated charge is explained by a relationship reminiscent of Formula (4). Only now we are dealing with the time intervals **Tp** and **Ta**, spent respectively on discharge and accumulation of charge; in other words, the interval of time between lightning bolts and the duration of the bolt:

$$Pp = Pa * Ta/Tp \qquad (5)$$

The smaller the time **Tp** of discharge, the greater the power

Pp will be generated during this discharge. Such power is called impulse power. Impulse power is large because the time of the discharge is about 0.01 second.

3. Artificial impulse devices are also able to generate colossal power for a short period of time. For example, a medium-sized radar can store energy in a special impulse capacitor for approximately half a second (0.5 sec), and discharge it in a matter of 30 microseconds (30* 10^{-6} sec). If the average power is 10 kilowatts, then the impulse power reaches the imposing value

$$Pp = Pa * Ta/Tp = 10,000 \text{ (w)} * 0.5/30*10^{-6} = 167 \text{ million watts.}$$

This is almost a third of the Dnieper Dam. And what a colossal construction that was? Radar only takes up the volume of a writing table.

The impulse power of laser devices, developed for the waging of the so-called "star wars" is much higher.

But even such modest and humorless creatures as electric eels (rays, catfish, and blackheads) can generate strong impulse power through gradually storing up energy in tens of thousands of special membranes located in their bodies. The electric fish slowly and undetectably grows energy in its membranes, waiting for its prey. The discharge of this energy is enough to knock a grown man off his feet. In the Brockhaus and Efron encyclopedia it is noted that *"the discharge current from a large, strong ray reaches 8 amperes, with a voltage of 300 volts.* This is enough power to light twenty four 100-watt light bulbs!

Doubtless, the liberation of psychic energy of living things in a short time brings about a greater emotional reaction than a gradual discharge. If a frog is thrown into boiling water, it will immediately jump out. But if the water starts off cold, and gradually gets heated to boiling, the frog won't experience painful shock, and will remain in the water until it cooks. The reaction of the frog to the impulse of administered pain differs from its reaction to a gradual administration of the same force.

One of the greatest pleasures accessible to humans is the sexual act. Its culmination, the orgasm, lasts in men for no longer than 1-3 seconds. But the shortness of this "impulsive" pleasure does not stop anyone. Men can court a woman and try to win her goodwill for a long time to experience this three-second pleasure and to cap off the process of courtship with a traditional conclusive phrase – rolling over and turning their back to their partner.

A sudden scare, as well as sudden joy is much a greater source of emotion than that same event spread out over a long time. It's logical to expect that the greatest pleasure from intellectual work will be reached at the moments of greatest emotional impulse. This pleasure is, as a rule, short-term. For this reason, the maximal value of **PSR** *the humor of elevation* is proportional not to the complexity **C** contained in the riddle of the joke, but to the magnitude of the impulse, the splash of emotion. This maximal value may be defined as the ratio of complexity **C** of the riddle to the time **Tp** spent on its solution:

$$PSR = C/Tp \qquad (6)$$

Formula (6) is the representation of a known phenomenon: a prolonged meditation over a difficult problem brings us far less pleasure than an immediate discovery of the answer.

The outstanding Russian philosopher **G. A. Golitzin** in his book *"Information and the Laws of Aesthetic Perception. – Knowledge, 1980"* came to the same conclusion (as the author was infomed by **Victor Shekotihin**):

*"Usually there exist various limitations which restrict immediate and full realization of this equilibrium, so that the push to the minimum **J** in reality turns into the subject's push for receiving the maximal influx of information:*

Humor Theory

$$E = {}_{\Delta}J/{}_{\Delta}t = max$$

where ${}_{\Delta}J$ = informativeness of the stimulus (comical), and

${}_{\Delta}t$ = its duration

An approach towards the target of perception, a decrease of J is accompanied by positive emotions, and a retreat from the target, by negative emotions. For this reason, E is an expression for emotions."

A good joke must contain the maximal complexity which the listener can solve in a short period of time.

Then the ratio of complexity to duration (intellectual pleasure, **PSR**) will be maximal. An impulsive, short-termed elevation of the mood causes a strong positive emotion. Externally this emotion is expressed through a smile or laughter. This then is the riddle of the funny. As we expected, it proved to be elementary and even primitive.

The final, seventh (that magic number 7!) formula, which dots all the 'i's, looks as follows:

$$EH = PE * C/Tp + BM, \qquad (7)$$

where **C** is the complexity of the riddle, and
Tp is the time spent on its solution.

This is the formula of laughter.
We found it!

Notice that **C** has the units of L*sec, and **Tr** is a measure of time (seconds). We have to agree that with any values of **C** and **Tp,** their quotient will be within the limits of 0.0 L to +0.5 L. This limitation will prove useful in the following analysis.

Formula (7) is simple but not obvious. Its simplicity calls up an internal protestation. Can it be that the solution of a sim-

ple riddle of the type contained in the following epigram by
Dorothy Parker:

> *Life is a glorious cycle of song,*
> *A medley of extemporanea,*
> *And love is a thing that can never go wrong*
> *And I am Marie of Roumania.*

brings greater pleasure than completing a crossword puzzle or
solving a mate-in-three chess puzzle?

To answer this question, let us conduct an elementary numerical analysis.

Let's compare the emotional effect of two intellectual problems: one difficult, and one simple. The first demands a strong
concentrated mental effort; the second is far more trivial. For
the first task, let's choose the composition of some funny
poem, for example a parody or an epigram. Like solving a
chess puzzle or taking a non-trivial integral, this problem is
difficult. Not everyone can grasp it. We will evaluate its difficulty $C1$ as an arbitrarily chosen 1.0L * sec. As the second
task, let's use the reading or apprehension of this same epigram
by the reader. Anyone can handle this. The complexity $C2$ of
this intellectual exercise we will evaluate more modestly. Let
$C2 = +0.01$ L * sec, that is 100 times less than $C1$. According
to the famous poet-parodist **Igor Yuzhanin**
(http://www.lebed.com/uzhanin/uzhanin-parodii.htm, in Russian), the time he spends composing an epigram is anywhere
between 2 minutes and 2 hours. The level of satisfaction he has
from composing a successful epigram, Yuzhanin evaluates as
quite high.

An epigram dedicated to one of the more arrogant participants of the particular chat room was composed in $T1 = 15$
minutes:

> As to the toilet, I'll dash to the forum
> Where I've already raised a formidable stench.

Humor Theory

Like a purga, I'll disturb the decorum
As though with a purger, if you pardon my French.

Kak v tualet, na forum zabegu,
gde mnoy uzhe ispisani vse steni
i, vipuchiv glaza, gonyu purgu.
Prichem, vse tchastche –s pomost'yu purgena.

Reading this epigram takes 8-10 seconds, and the time **T2** spent on solving the riddle contained in it, the finding of the pun *"purga-purger"* and the non-correspondence of those words is no more than one second.

Let us evaluate the **PSR** for these two cases:

Case 1:

$$PSR2 = +C1 / T1 = +1.0 / 900 = +0.0011 \text{ (L)}.$$

Case 2:

$$PSR2 = +C2 / T2 = +0.01 / 1 = +0.01 \text{ (L)}.$$

We see that with an incomparable complexity of the problems under question, the apex of intellectual pleasure from <u>reading</u> the epigram is about 9 times higher than the pleasure received from <u>composing</u> it. Therefore, while reading, our mood has much greater chances of rising past the level which brings about a burst of laughter, or at least a smile. This conclusion is confirmed by experience. Many of us have written successful bits of poetry and/or prose. But how often does the author laugh, composing his piece? On the other hand, people easily laugh at simple jokes.

At the same time, the character to whom the present epigram was dedicated received no pleasure from its reading. The hero of the epigram let loose a flood of profanity on the author, accusing of worthlessness, calling him naught else but Pidar'

Govlyanin (Peer Turdicus). The **PE** of the epigram's hero was obviously close to -1.0. Soon after, he left the chat room.

The provided explanation and the reverse proportionality of the intensity of pleasure of the time spent solving the "riddle" might seem simplified and mechanical. But this position is well confirmed by everyday practice. Even extremely pleasant information conveyed over the course of 10 minutes causes a smaller reaction than a small but sudden surprise.

A similar phenomenon is known to us from physiology. It is an established fact that the reaction of a nerve to an irritation is maximal in the initial period. In a short time, the nerve gets tired, and ceases reacting to the excitation.

It is entirely probable that people are endowed with humor as a mental ability of using this physiological phenomenon. Physiology gives one more confirmation that humor is a nearly reflexive, primitive feeling.

Let us continue the analogy between the processes of the apprehension of humor and the physical processes in impulsive systems.

Every impulsive process includes three phases:

1. an accumulation of energy;
2. a signal to discharge;
3. the discharge of the stored energy.

To develop the necessary impulse power in the process of discharge, it must first be accumulated.

In storm clouds, the accumulation of energy, as we mentioned above, happens gradually, through a slow migration of charge into the upper atmosphere. This is the first phase.

When the cloud has gathered the necessary, critical amount of energy, phase two begins. At the base of the storm cloud, a luminous discharge appears – a leader. It travels to the earth with enormous speed and blazes the way (creates a channel).

The third phase: The main body of the discharge – the lightning – travels down the created channel.

In impulse-based devices, the same things happen. During the first, the longest phase, a gradual accumulation of energy in special capacitors or magnetic spools, solenoids, occurs. In the second phase, a special device, a magnetron or klystron, is keyed with a short signal, and opens a path for discharging the stored energy. In the third phase, the stored energy discharges through the "opened" device.

If the second phase – the process of opening the discharge device – is lengthened, the discharged energy will be generated more slowly, and the maximal value of the power of the charge will be comparatively small. If the second phase happens before the end of the first phase, that is, the unlocking signal will come through when the energy has not yet been built up, then the maximal impulse power will be even less. If the first and second phases coincide, and the discharging device remains open during the charging process, then there won't be any accumulation of energy at all.

Every joke or anecdote are made and work completely analogously to impulse devices. The processes of the apprehension of humor include the same phases as the charge-discharge process.

This is how a typical narration of an anecdote and its apprehension by the listeners looks:

1. The listeners are told that they are about to hear something funny (**thesis 13**). This announcement causes a subconscious expectation of the forthcoming riddle, and the need for its solution. If the listener is not warned, the process of accumulation (in this case of information) might not happen. He will let the "salt" of the joke go in one ear, and out the other.

2. In the process of the narration, the listeners are told information formulating the "riddle". The listener takes in and stores this information. The accumula-

tion of information corresponds to the <u>first</u> phase: the process of the accumulation of energy in impulse devices.

3. A signal that the process of accumulation of information is complete follows; everything that the listener needs for solving the riddle has been conveyed to him, and the time has come to start on the "solution". This <u>second</u> phase is key. The signal to start the process is sometimes a word or a phrase; sometimes a pause. Humor researchers use the (quite technical) term "trigger" to designate this signal. As in impulse devices, this phase must be short. It must complete the process of accumulation.

Salvatore Attardo noted this fact, but did not follow it up with a convincing explanation. He analyzed 600 humorous passages (anecdotes, jokes) in Italian and English, dividing them into two categories: those relating to objects, and lingual (verbal) jokes. As can be seen from the table taken from his book (1994), jokes, in which the key word does not appear at the end, comprise no more than 4% of the total. We have only to guess whether this 4% corresponds to the unsuccessful models or to the category of the so-called *"soft humor"*.

Humor Theory

Table 2.9. Study A: Position of the key word (Disjunctor)

Humor	Object-based joke		Verbal joke		Total
	At the end	In the middle	At the end	In the middle	
Italian	251	11	34	4	300
American	231	4	60	5	300
Total	482	15	94	9	600

4. The next, <u>third</u> phase consists of the listeners' trying to solve the "riddle" which comprises the subject of the anecdote. As we already know, the time **Tp** allocated for the solution should be short. The correlation of the complexity **C** of the "riddle" to the estimated time **Tp** of its solution should be maximal. If the joke is told in a group of people, it is necessary that everyone or at least the majority of the people comprehend it simultaneously. In this case, a cumulative effect is achieved, and the effect from the narration of the anecdote increases by many times. A competition of a sort occurs in which the winners are those who laugh first, and the losers - those who get it a bit later. This competition plays a big part in the elevation or degradation of the social status of the listeners, expressed by the value **EH**. The biggest **EH** is gained by those with a good sense of humor, and the smallest by those who didn't understand the anecdote at all.

From formula (7) it follows that the time **Tp** is a critical element of any joke or anecdote. A skilled narrator constructs his jokes in such a manner that this time be as short as possible.

For this, we need to observe two conditions:

1. The key word (trigger, disjunctor, punch line) or the concluding pause must be located as closely as possible to the end of the joke. Then the listeners understand that the joke is finished, the "riddle" is formulated, and it's time to start the process of solution. If the key word is separated from the end of the joke by a few words, one of the following happens:

   a. the listener is at a loss as to what exactly the "riddle" is; which parts relate to its conditions, and which parts can be safely ignored.
   b. the time spent solving the riddle increases, and the effect of the joke is reduced.

An overly simple joke has a low level of complexity, and thus a small impulse of pleasure, or burst of **PE**, over the base level of the mood. Such a joke is quite justly called flat. An overly complex joke has a level **C** which can lead to a disproportional increase in **Tp**. The time **Tp** of a complex joke is hard to predict, and we cannot rely on its success with assurance. In this case, the level of **PE** may turn out to be low.

Moreover, overly complex jokes inevitably lead to a lack of synchronicity in their apprehension by the audience. Some are already beginning to laugh while others are opening and shutting their eyes in confusion, or straining their foreheads in concentration. This leads to a decrease of the level of **BM**. As a simple, so an overly complex joke has a value of **EH** smaller than optimal. The levels of **PSR** and **BM,** which are part of Formula (7), decrease. The value of **PSR** decreases due to an increase in time **Tp**. The **BM** decreases because there is no simultaneous group apprehension of the joke. All of this follows from Formula (7).

The time spent on solving the problem is usually 1-2 seconds. For simplified analysis, let's hold this value constant.

Then the success of the joke depends on the correct choice of value for **C**.

A successful joke contains a maximally complex problem which can be solved in a matter of 1-2 seconds.

From our determination, it is evident that the effect **EH** from any joke is subjective. It is determined by the prior knowledge base of the listeners, their ability to solve mental problems, but is expressed at the end with an elevation or a deprecation of the social status of the participants of the humoristic process: the narrator and his audience.

The skill of the narrator, the writer, the humorist consists in choosing the optimal complexity appropriate for the majority of his audience. Humor, like other art forms, is targeted at different groups, which can solve concrete riddles and uncertainties: plain folks, professionals, national groups, the elite, scholars, children, etc.

The graph shown below illustrates the process of apprehension of a one dimensional joke. By one-dimensional we mean a joke which contains only one "riddle" the solution of which brings us pleasure.

A multilevel joke may include several layers of one or two forms of humor. Let us look at an example:

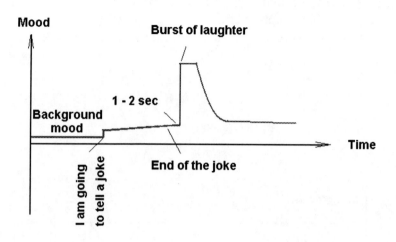

At the zoo:
- *Dad, is this monkey a man or a woman?*
- *That's a male.*

At the next cage:
- *Dad, is this one a man?*
- *Remember son: a man is someone with money! That one's a male!*

This anecdote is apprehended differently by different people. A "Nouvo Riche" will see it as a one-dimensional anecdote; he will deem himself a "man" and this will elevate his sense of superiority over others. The value of his **PE** will be high. Someone who is not a "Nouvo Riche" feels hostility towards them. Educated people will understand the bi- or even the multi-layeredness of the anecdote. Their **PE** will also have a high value. In the first place, they will laugh at the nonconformity of the "scientific" determination of the sex of the monkey. In the second place, they will feel intellectually superior over the boorish hero of the joke. In the third place, the listener might develop associations that in "Nouvo Riche" impotence is

109

nearly a professional disease. And so forth.

A graphical apprehension of this joke is shown on the graph below. Here you can see several bursts of pleasure.

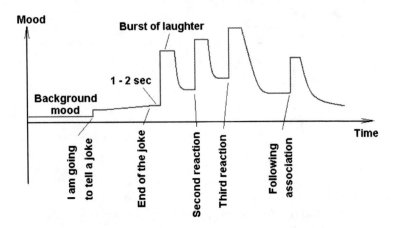

And here is how we can illustrate the apprehension of a one-dimensional joke by the narrator, the audience, and the person who is ridiculed:

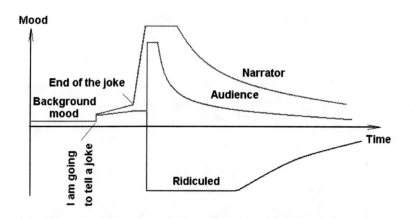

The author is grateful to **Miroslav Voinarovsky** and **Valentin Mamishev** for the fruitful discussion which allowed him to direct his attentions to a significant obstacle. Very frequently the reader laughs at a joke which touches on his religious or political persuasions. However, according to our prior reasoning, this should not happen. We have arrived at the conclusion that any joke with a negative value of **PE** should lead to a negative reaction. One of the reasons why a positive reaction happens anyway lies on the surface. By ways of experimentation and observation, it was determined that a person laughs at those "blasphemous" jokes which don't seriously offend him.

But it also happens that a joke of that sort both causes laughter and at the same time offends the listener.

The author conducted a special study, trying different, including borderline jokes with various audiences. Here is what was established. The first reaction – laughter – happens before the listener understands what the joke he just heard really means. At first he laughs at the pleasure of having solved the "riddle". And only moments later does he "get" the real meaning. After this, his mood quickly worsens. This "bipolar" process may be illustrated with the following graph:

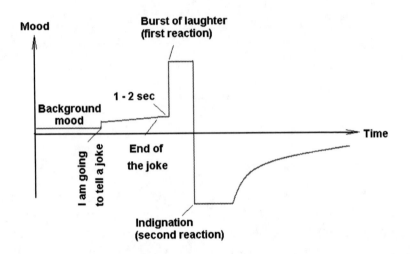

Before we begin the detailed deconstruction of the following examples, we will allow ourselves to remind the reader that all of the conclusions arrived at were based on either experimental data, or on prior conclusions with which the majority of researchers agree. The suggested theory does not factually contradict any of the existing theories of humor, and instead unites them, makes peace among them. In its derivation, the methods and approaches of the natural sciences were used to the greatest degree. We think that we have not left a single question unanswered.

The conclusions drawn in this work are easily checkable. To do this, one will not need expensive equipment or powerful computers. The subject of study is accessible to all.

Before we embark upon the experimental check of the theory, let us answer the following question, of interest to many:

Is it necessary for a person to have a sense of humor?

The answer to this question is ambiguous. Humor is a competition. A person who is not interested in this competition does not need a sense of humor. At this, he might be not stupider that his peers, but sometime much wiser. If a person doesn't understand humor, he is probably somewhat dull-witted. If he is not interested in humor, he is doubtlessly very wise or holds a high position which is difficult to shake.

The hero of the novel by **Somerset Maugham** *"The Moon and Sixpence"*, the brilliant painter Charles Strickland reached extraordinary heights of craftsmanship. Such great heights, that the opinion of those surrounding him were no longer of interest to him. He did not send his paintings to art shows or galleries, and at the end of his life, simply destroyed them. For Strickland, the knowledge of his own genius and understanding of the secrets of mastery of the arts was enough. But how many among us don't need daily supplements for our egos? Not very many at all. And that means, dear readers, that you and I are foredestined to humor, to jokes, teasing, anecdotes, cartoons and parodies.

Let's try to make our peace with this.

And let's move on to checking the theory. This will be a numerical verification, the first attempt in history to check the harmony of humor with algebra.

Chapter Six

Experimental Verification

Let us begin the experimental verification of the proposed theory. In this chapter we will numerically analyze examples of humoristic texts, jokes, and anecdotes. The selected texts will be changed for the purpose of decreasing or increasing the components in Formula (7). To simplify the analysis, let us simplify Formula (7) by holding the value of **Tp** accepted in the previous chapter constant. Let it be equal one second. That is we will analyze the riddles that the reader can solve in about 1 second. The value of **BM** we shall set to zero, as the only our audience is the reader. We get:

$$EH = PE * C, \qquad (8)$$

All of the selected texts have undergone the test of time and are either currently considered funny or were funny in the past. Almost all of them have been borrowed from humoristic anthologies.

Igor Krichtafovitch

Example # 1

Let us analyze a political anecdote. In this example, we will change only one constituent of formula (8) – the **PE**, leaving the value **C** constant:
C = const. PE = var.

"What is the difference between Jesus and the general secretary of the Soviet Communist Party L. I. Brezhnev?"
"Jesus heals the dumb and the GenSec is as dumb as a heel."

Let us analyze the value of **EH** of this anecdote. During Brezhnev's lifetime, the **PE** of the reader was obviously not equal to zero. The powerlessness of the old GenSec affected the life not only of every Russian, but of most Americans. Soviet people were irritated that such a great country was ruled by a sick man with obvious speech defects. For an initial evaluation of **PE** let us imagine that we are Soviet Union citizens during Brezhnev's epoch, whom we actively dislike. Any ridicule of him carries a probable risk, but decreases his social status, thereby increasing our own. For the sake of the discussion let PE = +0.6. The value **C** also is not equal to zero. To understand the pun in the joke, one must not only be familiar with common idioms, but also have political and biblical knowledge. It would be reasonable to therefore take a value of C = +0.3 L * t. The overall evaluation of the quality of this anecdote will be equal to

$$EH = PE * C = +0.6 * 0.3 = + 0.18 \text{ L}$$

We remind our readers that the maximum possible evaluation is equal to +0.5 L. We however have evaluated this anecdote at 1/3 of the maximal value. The mark is quite high. The reader may think that even this mark is too high. The modern reader doesn't find it funny. Why? We made the admission

118

above that we live in the Soviet Union during Brezhnev's epoch. But Brezhnev has been dead for 23 years, ever since according to the expression of **Andrew Knishev** *"five golden ones were buried on the field of miracles in the land of fools."*

Therefore the **PE** for the modern reader or a foreigner never can rise to the nearly maximal level of +0.6. More likely, its value will only be a reflexion upon our past dislike towards the Soviet leaders, and will equal about +0.3.

The **EH** for us will be equal about +0.09 L, that is almost 6 times lower than the maximum value. And so we're not laughing; the joke was weak.

But let us continue our exercise. Let's exchange the name of the GenSec for the name of another political leader:

"What is the difference between Jesus and the chairman of the GDR Erich Honecker?"

"Jesus heals the dumb and the chairman is as dumb as a heel."

The "salt" of the anecdote is fully preserved, and **C** continues to be 0.3 L * t, but the joke is now **completely** unfunny. The **PE** in this anecdote is equal to zero. We care absolutely nothing about Honecker or his mental capabilities. The **EH** of this anecdote is inevitably equal to zero, despite its obvious linguistic, semantic, semiotic, and other characteristics.

And currently this is a perfect time to revive the funniness of this joke by replacing the name of the anecdote's hero to George W. Bush.

Example #2

In this example, we will change the other part of Formula (8) – **C** – leaving the value of **PE** constant.

C = var. PE = const.

An officer, seeing a cloth dyer at work, jeeringly asked him, pointing at his snow-white horse: "Can you dye it too?" "Sure can," the dyer answered, "if it survives the boiling."

Let us evaluate the **EH** of this anecdote. The **PE** depends on whose side the listener is: the officer's, or the clever dyer's. The content of the anecdote assumes that the positive character here is the dyer, and therefore, in democratic circles, for which this anecdote was created (not for an Officer's Club, after all!), the **PE** will be high. For the sake of the discussion, let PE = + 0.6. The value of **C** here isn't very high; it's not too hard to guess that the horse won't be able to survive the boiling temperature of 100°C. Let us assume C = 0.3 L * t. The **EH** will be equal to +0.18 L, almost three times smaller than the maximal value.

Though in the society of dyers this anecdote might have received a higher rating, especially if there was a regiment of cavalry staying next door.

Now let's try to change the text a little:

An officer, seeing a cloth dyer at work, jeeringly asked him, pointing at his snow-white horse: "Can you dye it too?" "Sure can," the dyer answered, "but why does the Officer need a cooked dyed horse?"

We only changed a part of the last phrase. But the task became more complicated. The hint (the word *"boiling"*) has disappeared. Now in order to evaluate the "riddle", the incongruity contained in this anecdote, the reader must have certain knowledge in the field of cloth dying. Otherwise, he'll have to quickly (very quickly!) understand that cloths are dyed at a high temperature. A clever listener will proceed with the assumption that the anecdote makes sense and that it is funny, and will convulsively search for the answer. This follows from **thesis 13**, chapter 5: *For best effect of the joke, the listener should be prepared (forewarned).*

If the listener is not acquainted with the technology of cloth dying, and is not forewarned that the story being told is a joke, he might simply not react. But if the listener is sure that there is a riddle and he can quickly come to a solution, then his reward in the form of intellectual triumph will be greater than in the prior case. We shall evaluate **C** at 0.4 L * t in this case. The effect of the joke will rise to EH = +0.24 L, assuming that **PE** remains the same. Read both of the variants over again. Which would you prefer to tell in a circle of friends?

Now let's try to do the opposite operation and decrease the value of **C**:

An officer, seeing a cloth dyer at work, jeeringly asked him, pointing at his snow-white horse: "Can you dye it too?" "Sure can," the dyer answered, "but only the hooves; my basin is small."

Oho! We've removed the riddle and decreased the value of C almost to zero. We still have a small incongruity, since the dying of the hooves presents no interest to the officer. We also have a sense of enmity towards the officer, a clear lack of desire to help him. But assuming the **PE** is still equal to +0.6, and giving **C** a value of 0.1 L*t, we get an anecdote with a completely insignificant effect (EH = +0.06 L), appropriate for telling only perhaps to an audience of children.

We can continue our work of simplifying the text, for example:

An officer, seeing a cloth dyer at work, jeeringly asked him, pointing at his snow-white horse: "Can you dye it too?" "Sure can," the dyer answered, "but only if it can survive a temperature of 40° at which I usually dye cloth."

There is no riddle here at all; C = 0 L*t. The story has flatlined.

Notice that first we increased the level of **EH** and then decreased it to zero with the same level of aggression or value of **PE**, that is performed the opposite operation of what we did

121

with Example #1.

Now it will be simple for us to analyze a more refined story cited by Sigmund Freud in his work.

Example #3

A prince was riding past his holdings and noticed a man standing in a field who looked a great deal like him. The prince stopped and asked:
"Did your mother ever serve in residency?"
"No, but my father did."

We shall give the brilliant analysis of the anecdote by A. Luk its due:

"The questioned man would have liked, of course, to put the insolent person who dared insult the memory of his beloved mother in his place – but the brazen individual was a prince who he didn't dare put down or offend if he didn't want to pay with his life for this vengeance. This might have meant stifling the offence internally, but luckily, a joke paved the way to take his revenge without risk, accepting this implication with the help of a technical unification move, and addressing it to the attacking prince. The effect of the joke is so determined here by tendency that in the presence of a witty answer we are inclined to forget that the question of the attacker is itself witty, due to the implication contained therein.

In the cited analysis by A. Luk we can see the same factors as in ours. We have a positive value **PE** (*revenge without risk*), a non-zero value **C** (*the implication in the answer*). We have almost everything. The only things we lack are a consideration of the time factor (the impulse action) and the product of **PE** and **C**.

From the point of view of our theory, the analysis is completely different. The value **PE** for the average listener will be

122

quite high. The story punishes the arrogance of the aristocrat and reveals the unjustness of the social divide, based on primogeniture.

The inequality of the positions of the participants of the verbal skirmish, the humiliation of the strong and his inability to punish the offender give us the opportunity to visually imagine the entire scene: the smirking of the retainers, the powerless fury of the prince, and the quiet triumph of the respectfully bowing subject. For the listener, the value of **PE** will be close to +1.0. The difficulty of the joke is also at the highest level. We have to know the ways of life of noblemen, their high-society hoodlumism in order to solve the problem in a short time. The value of **C** will be no less than 0.5 L * t. The value of **EH** will also be equal to the maximal value: +0.5L.

Example # 4

Let us compare an analysis of a "medical anecdote" conducted by Victor Raskin and Salvatore Attardo with the approach of the already well known to us theory:

Someone who was previously treated for some illness inquires about the presence of a doctor at the doctor's place of residence, with the purpose of being treated for a disease which manifests itself by a whispering voice. The doctor's wife (who is young and pretty) answers (whispering, as the patient) that the doctor is not at home, and invites the inquirer to enter in the house.

From the point of view of Victor Raskin's theory, this text fits under the heading of the funny. It satisfies the "necessary and sufficient conditions" of the semantic theory of humor, specifically:

1. The text possesses an incompatibility, partial or full (in the given case: doctor/lover);

2. The two parts of the text are opposite in a certain sense (here: the presence or absence of sex).

But is this text funny? Clearly not. Why? Previous theories were not able to answer this question. Our theory does. Let us try to evaluate the values of the coefficients in Formula (7). First let's determine the value of **PE**. The listener of the above story does not get a sufficient impression of the personalities of the doctor and the patient. He can guess that the doctor is much older than his wife and doesn't satisfy her physically. But the listener is uncertain whose side to take: the cuckolded husband or the patient who unexpectedly got lucky, or maybe even, with a touch of maliciousness, the side of the flighty wife? The layout of the anecdote doesn't form a preference in the reader.

Most importantly, the anecdote is told unskillfully; the "punch line" is practically nonexistent. Because of that, the time **Tp** is prolonged, the riddle's resolution is spread over a long period of time, and the burst of emotions doesn't happen. For these reasons, the values of **PE** and **PSR** of this text are small. Their product, **EH**, is also small.

Let's change the text:

A patient goes into the residence of a doctor, who practices from home. The patient suffers from bronchitis. He talks in a whisper. He rings the doorbell. The doctor's wife, pretty and young, well known for her easy behavior opens the door. The patient whispers: "Is the doctor home?" The doctor's wife thinks that one of her young men has come to her, hoping for her favor. She takes his whisper as conspiratorial. She whispers in return: "Fortunately the doctor isn't home; come in quickly, and I'll give myself to you."

All of the "scripts" determining according to Raskin the presence of the funny remain in place. But something is missing here. The riddle here is toned down to be very simple ($C \approx 0$), and the time **Tp**, allowed for the solution, is stretched out over the whole text of the anecdote. We may as well stop expecting a burst of emotions, it's not going to happen.

Now we admit to the reader that we have tricked him a little, and analyzed not the "medical anecdote" itself, but its semantic analogy given by Salvatore Attardo. Here is how the anecdote really sounds:

"Is the doctor at home?" the patient asked in his bronchial whisper. "No," the doctor's young and pretty wife whispered in reply. "Come right in." ???

In this text, the complexity of the riddle rises to the maximum. The key to its solution is stated at the end, and expressed with a minimal amount of words. Thus the Pleasure of Solving the Riddle (**PSR**) here is much higher than in the texts cited above, equal in semantics and informativeness. This anecdote is doubtlessly funny.

The reader has the opportunity to independently vary the text of <u>Example #3</u> so as to change the values of **PE, C,** and **Tp**. Try to tell the obtained variants in different social groups, and compare the effects of each.

As an exercise and simultaneous verification of the theory, we will allow ourselves to provide a few relatively little-known comic opuses. We remind our readers that the values **EH, PE,** and **C** are always subjective, they are marks presented by you personally. Let's try to produce a qualitative evaluation of the coefficients which comprise Formula (8), and then to compare the chosen value of **EH** with the product of **C** times **PE**. To do this is not difficult; the entire analysis will take only several minutes. We will use a procedure consisting of three steps.

1. Let us evaluate the quality of the anecdote (the value of Effect of Humor (**EH**) by choosing one of 15 possible values provided in Table 1:

Table 1

Highest class	+0.4 or 0.5
I'll call my best friend immediately and tell him this joke	+0.3
I'll tell this joke tomorrow at work	+0.24
I'll have to remember this and tell it at an opportune moment	+0.2
A pleasant anecdote; I laughed	+0.18
It made me smile	+0.12 or 0.15
So-so	+0.09 or 0.1
Childish joke	+0.03 or 0.06
This isn't humor	0
Stupid anecdote	-0.05 or -0.1
Idiotic anecdote	0.15, -0.2, or -0.25
Why do they print this garbage?	-0.3, -0.4, or -0.5

Let's evaluate Personal Empathy (**PE**) using Table 2:

Table 2

The character(s) in the anecdote have a direct relation to me I could have been in their place I actively dislike such people, or one of the characters is my hero.	+1.0
I understand the actions and motivations of the characters well.	+0.6
I understand the psychology of the characters, but don't think I could have been in their place. Everything here has little to do with me.	+0.3
I don't care about the characters in the	0

anecdote	
I don't understand their actions.	
The anecdote caused unpleasant associations.	-0.5
One shouldn't joke like that about good people.	
An insulting, blasphemous anecdote.	-1.0

Let's evaluate the value of Complexity of the riddle **(C)**, using values from Table 3:

Excellent	Good	Not bad	So-so	Mediocre	Flat joke
0.5	0.4	0.3	0.2	0.1	0

Let's compare the product **PE* C** the reader came up with against your value of **EH.**

Example #5

A young actor is subbing for a sick partner in a play. He had no time to learn the part, so the director told him to follow the cues of the prompter.
The prompter cues: (Sits in the chair!)
The actor sits.
Prompter: Should I marry, perhaps?
Actor: Should I marry, perhaps?
Prompter: No, I suppose not.
Actor: No, I suppose not.
Prompter: (rises with difficulty).
Actor: It rises with difficulty!

The below two examples bear our marks which serve as our personal opinion.

EH = +0.15
PE = +0.3

$C = 0.4$
$PE * C = +0.12$
$EH/ (PE * C) = 1.25$

Example #6

A young lieutenant sees a drunken major in a restaurant, who is ineffectually trying to pick apart a chicken drumstick with a knife and a fork.

"Major," snidely says the lieutenant, a bird is eaten with the hands.

The major raises his head:

"And snot is wiped up with a sleeve!"

$EH = +0.2$
$PE = +0.3$
$C = 0.5$
$PE * C = +0.15$
$EH/ (PE * C) = 1.33$

We now move on to the most interesting part: practical exercises. The reader has the opportunity to conduct his own evaluation, based either on his tastes or on those of an imaginary audience. You can at least perform these calculations on jokes that appealed to you.

Example #7

"Why doesn't Margaret Thatcher wear mini skirts?"
"So that nobody sees her balls."

$EH =$
$PE =$
$C =$
$PE * C =$
$EH/ (PE * C) =$

Example #8

Nancy Reagan was an adherent of free distribution of oil to the poor population. She said: "Even poor people should have something to dip lobster tails into". (From the Johnny Carson show, February 1982).

EH =
PE =
C =
PE * C =
EH/ (PE * C) =

Example #9

A man and a woman on a first date:
"I'm from Texas, ma'am. In Texas, everything is bigger than anywhere else. We have the biggest buffalos, the tallest corn in the world. We have the most oil."
A little later, when they are in the bedroom the man continues: "And now you'll see what else Texans have that's bigger than anywhere else."
A minute later (in a wounded voice): "You should have warned me that you're from Texas too".

EH =
PE =
C =
PE * C =
EH/ (PE * C) =

Example #10

Ivan Krylov (Russian poet) had a sore on his leg which long prevented him from walking. With difficulty, he came out onto Nevsky Prospekt in San-Petersberg. A tactless friend was riding by, who could find nothing better than to yell: "What, did the sore pass?" "Just now," unhesitatingly replied Ivan Andreevich.

EH =
PE =
C =
PE * C =
EH/ (PE * C) =

Example #11

The first earthly expedition landed on Mars. Martians surrounded their ship, and a lively exchange of information was begun. After some fundamental notions were discussed, a question about reproduction arose. A Martian male and female coupled immediately and a baby Martian appeared. After that, a human man and woman took off their spacesuits and showed how this is done on Earth. When they again put on their suits, the Martians couldn't hold back their confusion: "Where is the little human?" They were explained that the baby will appear in 9 months. The Martians: "So why was he in such a hurry towards the end?"

EH =
PE =
C =
PE * C =
EH/ (PE * C) =

Example #12

At one party, a pretty female crab saw an unusual male. He walked not like other crabs – sideways – but straight. "What an unusual crab," the female thought, "I mustn't let this op-

portunity go by." She went up to him and offered to get married. The crab immediately agreed. In the morning, the new wife saw her spouse moving around just like all the other crabs. "Beloved," she asked through tears, "why do you walk today not like yesterday, but like all of the others?" "But my dear," answered the newlywed, "I can't get that drunk every day."

EH =
PE =
C =
PE * C =
EH/ (PE * C) =

Example #13

A husband and wife, both passionate golfers are chatting over a cup of tea. "Tell me, love, if I die, will you marry another woman?" "Well, to be honest, that's entirely possible." "What, and she will sleep in our bed?" "My dear, what is so unusual in that? Yes, she will sleep in our bed; where else would she sleep?" "And she will drive my car?!" "That's also not impossible. I don't rule out that she may drive your car." "And will she play with my golf clubs?!!" "Oh, no!!! She's left-handed."

EH =
PE =
C =
PE * C =
EH/ (PE * C) =

Example #14

Tiger Woods stopped his Mercedes at a remote gas station for refueling. An old man helped him to fill the tank. When

Tiger leaned toward the nozzle, two tees fell out of his pocket. "What are those?" - asked the old man. "I place my balls on them when I drive" - answered Tiger. "Whoa! Those people at Mercedes think of everything".

EH =
PE =
C =
PE * C =
EH/ (PE * C) =

Example #15

Magister: Enumera pronomina duo!
Discipulus: Quis, ego?

EH =
PE =
C =
PE * C =
EH/ (PE * C) =

Example #16

"Do you know what NIS of former Soviet Union stands for? Network of Ineffectual Schmucks."
(from comic show in Israel).

EH =
PE =
C =
PE * C =
EH/ (PE * C) =

Find the average value of **EH/ (PE*C)** that you analyzed. To do this, divide the sum of all the **EH/ (PE*C)** values by the number of problems analyzed. If the average value is significantly different from one, try to analyze why this happened: a) you're not sure that you were able to evaluate these examples objectively, b) you made your decisions too hastily, or c) you were guided by a subconscious desire to discredit the proposed theory.

The author has gone through this process with examples ##5-16 and received an average value of **EH/ (PE*C)** = 1.25 L. The maximum deviation was 1.33, and the minimum was 0.7. Taking into account the subjective character of the coefficients in Formula (8), the obtained average divergence should be recognized as satisfactory.

The author would be grateful to those readers who would take it upon themselves to do these simple exercises and share their results. Your input will help refine the proposed theory.

Chapter Seven

Abstract Anecdotes

Abstract anecdotes appeared relatively recently and are probably a Russian phenomenon. When these anecdotes first appeared, they produced a dual impression, at first seeming completely non-witty. But with time, this type of humor became more common and used to cause the same collective laughter as traditional anecdotes. And still a feeling of awkwardness has never left the author. He laughed but has never completely understood why. What's funny about the following anecdotes?

Example #17

*Two cabinet makers in a bath. One says "Pass the soap",
and the other says,
"What am I, a bowling ball?"*

Example #18

A worm is riding his bicycle in the winter; he looks and sees: on the electric cables between two posts there's a cow swinging. He gets off the bicycle, feels his tires, and says: "spring is coming."

We must acknowledge that the developed theory was not immediately capable to explain why these abstract anecdotes are funny. They did not have the characteristic that's inherent in the funny. They lack the riddle, the uncertainty, the "shining contradiction" which is to be resolved in the usual anecdote so as to receive pleasure from this mental concentration, which leads to bursts of laughter. But these anecdotes are laughed at, laughed at genuinely; which means that there's something to them. And this something needs explanation; otherwise our theory will be hung out to dry.

Let's analyze the following anecdote:

Example #19

A brick crawls along the wall and sees a calendar.
"What's the time?" asks the brick.
"Wednesday," replies the calendar.
"Hooray!" rejoiced the brick.
"Summer's coming soon!"

In a regular anecdote, the confusion caused by a dialog between a brick and a calendar would have been deciphered in the last phrase, and deciphered logically. All of the ends would have come together. Here, all of the threads remain loose. There is no reason or logic.

We will try to approach the analysis of this class of anecdotes like we have before. Generalizing the facts:

- The abstract anecdote exists. This is a reality.
- It brings its listeners pleasure. Genuine pleasure.
- This class of anecdotes is for the prepared listener.

We might suppose that the listeners tired of the usual anecdotes, and there was demand for something new, something extravagant, as it happened in poetry, art, and music.

Innovations in the arts are created initially for the elite, the experts "oversated" with the customary forms. If an unprepared reader flips open a compilation of futurist poet **Velimir Khlebnikov**, he will very soon... shut it. Iambic tetrameter is so much more agreeable.

If a person wishing to become an enthusiast of paintings begins his career with the canvases of **Picasso** or **Gauguin**, he will hardly find in their works repose for his soul. He will be drawn to **Shishkin**, **Repin**, and **Raphael**. Likewise with contemporary forms of classical music. The reader who's been to at least one concert of modern music will agree that this is perhaps the only thing that can't be termed a "quiet horror." **Wagner** and **Tchaikovsky** are incomparably better.

But the professionals and real enthusiasts may have "surpassed" the traditional arts; they have exhausted the classics, they are bored. They aren't interested in Rafael or **W. Shakespeare**. They are sated with Rafael's *"Madonna"*, *"Romeo and Juliet"*, and *"The Nutcracker"*. They want new forms.

In humor, the abstract anecdote became such a form. It would be easiest of all to define **the abstract anecdote as a meaningless anecdote**.

But such a definition won't help explain why people laugh at these anecdotes and laugh in the right place, that is, simultaneously. It is precisely in this simultaneity that we will search for the key to their understanding.

As we saw in Chapter 5, all anecdotes are built according to a standard scheme. In each one there's a moment that the listeners await, afraid to miss it. This is the denouement, the concluding phrase or word. This is followed by a short pause, during which the listeners search for an answer to the "riddle", the salt of the anecdote.

The abstract anecdote has all these elements except one: there is no solution. But the experienced listener knows that there *must* be a solution, and that he can find it in 1-2 seconds. But he doesn't find it. And then... he understands that **there is no solution**; that he was slipped a cleverly fabricated surrogate. And he laughs. At what, at himself, that he was so cleverly fooled? Let's go back two phrases: *"the listener understands"* – there it is! The riddle is not that it doesn't exist at all, but that it doesn't exist **there** where it should have been in a real anecdote. The listener finds an empty space and gleefully points: *"Here it is, here is where the salt of the anecdote should be! I recognized the spot! I'm a real expert in humor!"*

We'll believe this listener that anecdotal art for the sake of art has a right to exist. The author candidly admits that abstract anecdotes don't hold a special place in his heart.

Now we can give a deeper explanation. **"The salt of an abstract anecdote consists of the lack of meaning <u>there where</u> in regular anecdotes the meaning is found."**

Abstract anecdotes are humor built upon humor. For military anecdotes the foundation is the life and work of soldiers; for salacious jokes – sex, in all of its manifestations. The nourishment source for abstract anecdotes is humor itself. They are built on humor, and on humor, it may be said, they parasite.

But not all authors and users of abstract anecdotes share this point of view. With chagrin we have to admit that under the headings of abstract anecdotes regular ones are seen more and more frequently. They are connected to abstract anecdotes not through structure, but through secondary characteristics: bricks, hippopotami, cows, irons, and so on.

Humor Theory

We have not investigated abstract anecdotes in our prior analysis. The basics of our theory was developed before the birth of abstract anecdotes. But the theory proved to be capable of explaining even that which at first had not been a subject of analysis. It proved to be more universal than the object of investigations. And this inspires optimism.

Chapter Eight

Conclusion

Let us draw to a close. Already in the first pieces of writing left by our hoar ancestors we could see evidence that humor has been with us forever.

Humanity evolved, the sciences appeared, fields of knowledge: first the natural and then the engineering, and later, the philosophical. With the appearance of philosophy, the study of humor began. Not all of the ancient documents have reached us today, but those that have survived leave no doubt that the funny has always occupied the great minds of the founders and leading figures of knowledge of humans and societies.

Society moved forward; scholarly minds penetrated the secret depths of the human soul more and more. But concurrently with the development of the sciences about mankind, we saw the development of humor. The rough comedies of Aristophanes, which entertained the ancient Greeks turned into a refined art, behind whose clever veil it became harder and harder to discern the truth; the deeply rooted sources of our habit of laughing at those like ourselves. Many researchers thought that they unraveled the riddle of laughter, that they opened the curtain of the eternal and mystical art. But new researchers appeared and posed questions to which these prior theories could not give an answer.

Why does a person laugh? What does he laugh for? How do we formally define the difference between the funny and the unfunny? All these questions remained unanswered.

For an objective evaluation of the developed theory, let's remember what state the theory of humor was in prior to the present work. We'll entrust ourselves to the opinion of Salvatore Attardo as a most competent authority in the given question. Moreover, Dr. Attardo is the editor of the *International Journal of Humor Research,* and through his hands pass all of the publications for this highly representative publishing organization.

According to S. Attardo (1994), there are three groups of theories of the funny, specifically:

Table 1.2. Three groups of theories

Cognitive	Social	Psychoanalytical
Incongruity	Hostility	Release
Contrast	Aggression	Sublimation
	Superiority	Liberation
	Triumph	Economy
	Derision	
	Disparagement	

It will be completely apparent to those who have taken it upon themselves to become acquainted with the conclusions presented in this work and the conducted analysis that not one of these theories can answer the questions of interest to us due to the limitation in its scope. Answers can be found only if we look at all of the theories together, by finding their uniting beginning.

Salvatore Attardo, having taken it upon himself to learn all of the existing theories of humor has justly concluded that *"the theories examined in this book are either a partial development or an intuitive direction of research, and the analysis and conclusions drawn from these studies are little more than anecdotal."* At the same time, Attardo distinguishes the semantic theory (SSTH) of V. Raskin as a *"formal theory, which predicts and may be tested with the help of "hard facts"; therefore, a sort of consensus exists that SSTH is the most epistemologically powerful and promising theory that exists in the field of the linguistic study of humor."*

But at the same time he notes that V. Raskin himself evaluates his theory more conservatively. He thinks that a theory based on semantic differences is unable to give a qualitative evaluation to the subject of humor. We saw based on the example of the "medical anecdote" that this assertion is quite just.

Moreover, this theory does not even pose the task of answering the question: "why do people laugh?" In this sense the comparison of the semantic theory with the "theory" of magnets as bodies with poles seems quite natural.

The **presented theory of humor** gives an answer to all, as far as we can see, of the imaginable questions. The mystery of humor became simple and almost obvious. The concept developed doesn't contradict any of the existing theories. On the contrary, a unifying foundation had been found for everything written up to this point. The theory of humor rather unites the more obvious concepts and sciences into a simple and ordered logical system. Moreover, it is in agreement with the experimental data, information and facts from such exact sciences as genetics and physiology.

In the presented theory, the **purpose of humor** is formulated. A person's reaction to a joke or anecdote is determined not by the elegance of the phrasing a text, and not by its presentation, but only by that **elevation of his social status** within the group in which the joke is told.

Humor is a bloodless, contact-less intellectual **weapon**, given to mankind for elevating one's social status relative to his peers. This weapon can be used in direct intellectual combat when the goal is attaining superiority over the opponent; his degradation; victory in an intellectual duel. This same weapon can be used for more subdued mobility up the social ladder: attainment of attention and authority in the group. Finally it serves for attracting the attentions of the opposite sex which, as we saw, is inherent in the quite concrete genetic algorithm of human development.

When the purpose of humor is formulated, the **mechanism of the affect** of humor became quite specific. The narrator or author jokes to increase his own social status. The joke must be constructed and presented in such a way that the status of the listener also increases, and the status of the object of ridicule decreases. Any example of humor is either a **jibe**, with intent to demean its target and elevate the status of the others at his cost, or an intellectual **riddle**, elevating the status of those who solved it.

A riddle, comprising the foundation of any example of the **humor of elevation**, must have an optimal complexity so as to be solved in a **short period of time**. In this case, the **impulse of emotions** reaches a maximal value. The **pleasure** gained from solving an intellectual riddle, which is **connected** to the elevation in social status, leads to a burst of emotions expressed through **smiles, laughter, or howling**.

An unconditional merit of the proffered theory is the fact that it doesn't introduce new terminology, and does without value conceptualizations. Humor is a primitive emotion, and its nature is explained with the simple-most means. An elementary **mathematical apparatus** has been created, allowing us to perform a **quantitative assessment** of the effect of humor.

Chapter Nine

To Be Continued...

So what's next? It would seem that there are no more un-answered questions, and the veil comprising the mystery of humor has been lifted forever.

It turns out that the basic tenets of the present work have broader applications.

In the first place, this relates to such fine arts as **humoristic prose**. While reading humoristic novels, narratives, or short stories, the reader bursts into laughter rarely. However while reading, he receives pleasure different from the sort that he receives while reading serious literary works. The developed theory allows us to conduct a detailed examination of humoristic works with a quantitative analysis of each episode in which the Effect of Humor (**EH**) is non-zero.

Clearly, many episodes of soft humor have a cumulative effect targeted at a gradual elevation of the overall level of emotions. A constant solution of simple riddles sprinkled through the text of a humorous work; the juxtaposition of the reader's ego with the bumbliness of the characters of the story contribute to an Increase of the Social Status of the reader and his self-image. It is evident that such an analysis of existing humoristic texts is the natural next step for the **presented theory**.

In the second place, it would be natural to apply this theory to the **art of versification**. How is poetry different from prose? Only in two ways: rhyme and rhythm. Neither of these characteristics bears an inherent substantive load. But the perception of poetry is strikingly different from the perception of prosaic texts. Why?

Vitaliy Bernstein in his eminent article *"What is Poetry"* (www.Lebed.com, N390, in Russian) wrote: *"If in prose, as Alexander Pushkin correctly noted, the most important distinctions are precision and clarity, then a lyrical poem is frequently characterized by a certain mystery; an incompleteness. And this gives it additional charm.*

But what is this charm?

Let's take an example. Are the following words capable of touching the reader:

"In Israel, performances of Wagner's works are not welcomed, but you and I will go off on our own and listen to his operas, despite the fact that somewhere nearby there are class earth-sky rockets standing at ready, and someone is preparing an armored attack.

Touching, but…it doesn't touch. The same words by meaning, having been re-written in verse are perceived entirely differently:

> Let Stingers be aimed at the sky,
> Let tanks be in prelusion,
> To the Nuremberg Mast'rs you and I
> Will listen in seclusion.

Igor Krichtafovitch

Pust' v nebo napravleni "stingeri"
I kto-to sidit na brone,
Mi "Bremenskie meistenzingeri"
Poslushaem naedine.

Let's remember the quotation of **Leibniz** cited in the second half, that *"music is the rejoicing of the soul, which calculates, without knowing it itself."* Could the same thing be happening at the apprehension of poetry? Certainly.

Poetical lines are apprehended by our brain just like jokes. The brain calculates the rhythm of the poem, thus performing a simple intellectual task. We compare the rhythm, the size of every line with the corresponding one, repeating this rhythm. We catch rhymes at the end of the lines and relate them to rhymes in the corresponding lines. The measures and rhymes may be simple, but the level of intellectual work in the apprehension of poetry is much higher than it is at the apprehension of prose. This happens not because of the difficulty of the mental labor, but because of its rapidity. While reading prosaic works, this labor doesn't occur at all. But when reading the simplest iamb or chorea, we demand constant concentration of our brain. A successful apprehension of poetry, the comparison of stresses and rhymes dome in a short time brings us additional pleasure. It would be quite logical to allow that the pleasure from the apprehension of poetical rhythms and measures is not added but is multiplied by the pleasure of apprehension of the meaning of the poem. Formula (3), suggested in Chapter 5, may be used for illustrating the process of apprehending poetry:

$$EP = PMR * PM, \qquad (9)$$

Where **EP** is the Effect from the apprehension of the Poem, **PMR**- the Pleasure from the apprehension of Measures and Rhymes; and **PM** – Pleasure from apprehending the Meaning.

We'll note that the multiplication sign explains the manifold strengthening effect of the poem in comparison to prose where PMR is equal to zero. Therefore even a simple poetical rhythm and an unassuming rhyme can bring us pleasure. That's why, as **Valeriy Lebedev** said in the article *"What to the Cicadas Sing About"* (Lebed, #388, www.lebed.com, in Russian), *"poetry may permit itself to be a little stupid, even completely dumb, and be limited to syllabic graces."* High value of **PMR** compensates for the low value of **PM.**

If we become acquainted with a large number of poetical works, the intellectual work of perceiving rhyme and rhythm becomes automatic. The recognition of simple measures no longer brings us such pleasure. Banal rhymes such as "cat" – "mat" are easily anticipated by the trained mind and begin to irritate the reader, not bringing him the expected pleasure. The oversated reader demands more complex mental exercises. He gets bored with iambic tetrameter. In response to this demand, more complex poetical forms crop up; fresh, more unexpected rhymes are sought, following the first and recognition of the second increases the complexity of that intellectual riddle which the reader constantly solves while reading poetry. This is what comprises the "magic words" of poetry, which are frequently ascribed mysterious characteristics. They are indeed mysterious, but only until an explanation for them is found. And the essence of the explanation is contained in Formula (9). The magic didn't disappear, though it became apparent.

It is clear that a creation of a logical theory of versification can be started with Formula (9) and finished with it, too. But in between these steps lies an immense world of work.

We quote another phrase by Vitaliy Bernstein: *"On the map of various forms of human creations, the ocean of poetry lies somewhere in the space between the continent of prose on one side, and of music on the other.*

Is our theory of humor applicable to the second continent, to music? **What is music** and how is it different from a disconnected set of sounds created by the same instruments?

What distinguishes music from cacophony?

As Valeriy Lebedev wrote in that same article: *"The element of music is sounds, organized according to their own laws of harmony, counterpoint, and other disciplines."*

Let us turn our attention to the words *"organized according to the laws"*. Music theory will tell us that a musical composition is built according to a "vertical" combination of sounds (the most important of which is the chord) and to a "horizontal" combination (melody, chord sequence, etc.).

From music theory we can glean much information about what laws the two kinds of combinations are built according to, about the principles of harmonic constructions (chords) and melodic (melodies) intervals. For example, we can learn that *"intervals, which divide sounds into chords can be consonant (octave, perfect fifth, perfect fourth, major third, minor third, sixth), dissonant (second, seventh, alteration of the consonants –i.e. an alteration of the tones of consonant intervals.)"* But most importantly, what music theory tells us about chords is that *"although a simultaneous sound of two tones of different pitches can also be viewed as a chord (double-stop), a normal chord should contain no less than three tones, and consequently, more than one interval.*

We see in this the key to understanding the harmonic construction and its apprehension by the listener. The sounds in a chord are separated by certain intervals. The human brain can catch these intervals and, most importantly, the relationship between them. If the human ear catches two tones, sounding simultaneously, it doesn't pick up on a pattern. But when a second tone is added, the brain has the opportunity to compare the intervals between the first and second tone, and the interval between the second and third tone and determine whether these intervals are equal or proportional. If the relationship between the intervals is logical and recognizable, the brain obtains pleasure from finding this logical ratio that sounds like a harmony. The pleasure from solving this tiny mental riddle is that same pleasure which we receive from a well-constructed chord.

Humor Theory

We now modify Formula (9) to use in connection with a musical composition, such as a song:

$$ES = PRI * PMR * PM, \qquad (10)$$

where **ES** is the Effect from apprehending the Song, and **PRI** is the Pleasure received from Recognizing musical Intervals.

If we assume that this formula adequately reflects the value of emotional elevation from listening to a song, we can see that the same multiplication sign explains why music, even with mediocre lyrics can bring great pleasure.

Of course, we can't explain the whole spectrum of the effects of music with Formula (10). We imagine that the developed approach will be a powerful instrument in the understanding of musical compositions. We'd like to hope that the developed approach will find followers capable of understanding the connection between musical tones, describing them mathematically, and developing a scientific (not descriptive) theory of music.

As for the study of **humor** itself, it seems quite evident that further formalization may provide the key to computer generation of humor as well as numerical evaluation of the quality of jokes and anecdotes. Of course, the latter is considered only as it pertains to a specific person, taking into account all of his knowledge, preferences and talents. A complete model of a person is unlikely and unjustifiably difficult, but a creation of a psychological cognitive profile of a person is entirely possible on the basis of a set of data comprised of a few hundred questions and answers of the type: *"What was the name of the Apostle Paul prior to his conversion?"* or *"what is your favorite sport?"*.

The book of **Alexander Luk** *"On the Sense of Humor and Wit"* caused in its time a very negative reaction of professional humorists. A well-known writer-satirist **Leonid Likhodeev** dedicated an annihilating article to it in the *"Literaturnaya Gazeta"*. People who loved and valued humor were bothered by the fact that a scientific study of the phenomenon of laughter will deprive it of its mysterious flair, and will eventually lead to a decline of the skill of making people laugh. The same fear was voiced by famous Russian comic writer **Michael Zhvanetsky.**

In the present work it was shown that humor has a primitive, almost reflexive nature. Knowledge of the patellar reflex won't help us simulate a nervous disease. Many men know well how the female body works, but this by no means decreases the number of those eager to possess it. The fears of L. Likhodeev and M. Zhvanetsky are, fortunately, needless.

On this note we conclude our narrative.

LaVergne, TN USA
06 April 2011
223146LV00001B/115/A